The Last of the
Mountain Men

Harold Peterson

Backeddy Books

B-7.69[H]

PRINTED IN THE UNITED STATES OF AMERICA

Library of Congress Catalog Card Number 68-57081

To ROLLAND and KAY,

PIONEERS MORE THAN THEY KNEW

To Walt Bingham

and most of all to Betty,

who helped in many ways

≪ To him who has once tasted the reckless independence, the haughty self-reliance, the sense of irresponsible freedom, which the forest life engenders, civilization thenceforth seems flat and stale. Its pleasures are insipid, its pursuits wearisome, its conventionalities, duties and mutual dependence alike tedious and disgusting. . . . The wilderness, rough, harsh, and inexorable, has charms more potent in their seductive influence than all the lures of luxury and sloth. And often he on whom it has cast its magic finds no heart to dissolve the spell, and remains a wanderer and an Ishmaelite to the hour of his death.

FRANCIS PARKMAN

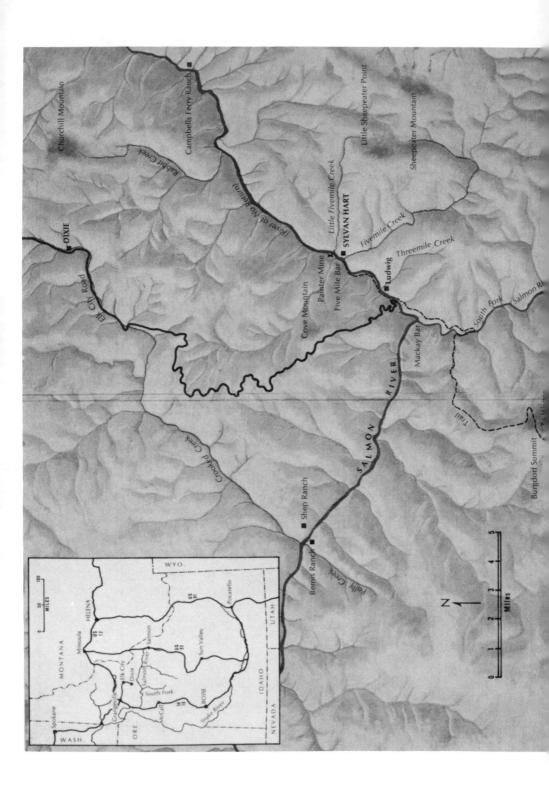

Preface

Since Harold Peterson wrote *Last of the Mountain Men* in 1969 enough changes have occurred at Five Mile Bar on the Salmon River in Idaho, without diminishing any curiosity about the man who lived there, that a reprint of the book, accompanied by a new foreword, seems justified.

At the time this book was first published, Sylvan Hart, also known as "Buckskin Bill," had not the notoriety that he subsequently gained. He had been living in the canyon for almost thirty years, alone much of the time—though not a hermit, even by an indulgent standard—and always busy, without running on a time-card. Hart's life may have been crosscurrent to the mainstream, but his intelligence, interests, and abilities ranked him as omnicompetent; there was little that he didn't savvy.

As the flow of newspaper, magazine, and television stories grew, so did his stream of visitors and mail. Backpackers, hikers, hippies in search of a guru camped on his place, and not infrequently abused his hospitality. By the mid-1970s summer regattas of jet-boats and rafts daily crossed the eddy to the beach in front of his cabin and disgorged their passengers to view "Buckskin Bill"—the "Old Faithful" of Salmon River.

In the spring it was evident that Hart enjoyed this attention: animated and good-humored as an otter, he held forth in his best "Darn the settlements, I say" Oklahoma drawl. He was curious about his visitors, their hometowns and occupations; he regaled the tourists, and although most of his remarks were well ballasted with facts, he wasn't above a little dude-stuffing now and then. Whatever else the folks thought, few of them left disappointed or disillusioned.

But by early fall Hart had tired of playing the "dancing bear;" the parade of visitors had left him spent; he needed the winter to revive. After August, boatmen spared him if they could.

In his "renowned" years, Hart traveled more frequently than he had in the past. He made trips to the Southwest, Iceland, and Russia; he also gave talks to school children, and often rendez-voused with fellow muzzleloaders at their regional matches.

One consequence of his increasing notoriety was the publicity given his dispute with the federal government over the owner-ship of Five Mile Bar. In the 1960s the U.S. Forest Service got the damp-eared notion that it should evict Hart from the Idaho Primitive Area within the Payette National Forest. His predica-ment was eventually resolved when the Forest Service discovered that it did not even own the bar—the five acres had been patented as a millsite associated with the Painter mine across the river. Rodney Cox, mentioned in the book as Hart's nephew, obtained title to the millsite from a third party, and in 1974 gave Sylvan a deed to four-tenths of an acre. In 1977 the USFS offered Hart $35,000 for his holding; he refused it.

Mr. Cox moved to the bar with his wife and family in the 1970s and built an incongruous yellow house on the otherwise rustic site. In 1976-1977 Cox also decided to charge river outfitters $200 for summer "visitation" privileges at Five Mile Bar. Most outfitters were put off by the scheme, but Hart apparently threw in with it. Then in 1977 the Cox's oldest boy was killed at the bar when he fell beneath a vehicle being used to haul firewood. Shortly thereaf-ter the Cox family left the Salmon River for a channel of their own.

On April 28, 1980, a jet-boat pilot from Mackay Bar (a guest ranch three miles downriver), visited Hart and found that he wasn't feeling well; the pilot promised to check on him the following day. Said Sylvan, "When you come back, I'll either be better or I'll be dead." Returning the next morning, the boatman found Hart dead on his cot.

The burial took place at Five Mile Bar a few days later. Two dozen persons were present: Hart's three sisters, two of his nephews, friends from Grangeville and the Salmon River canyon. His pine coffin, flag-covered, was lowered into the grave that had been dug at the river-end of his garden. Three friends fired a salute with Hart's own long rifles.

A month later a dozen friends returned to mark the grave with a granite tombstone:

Sylvan A. Hart

"Buckskin Bill"

May 10, 1906   April 29, 1980

The Last of the Mountain Men

Erected by his Friends, the Ee-da-how Long Rifles, June, 1980

Hart left his estate to his nephew, Rodney Cox. Cox offered to sell the Five Mile Bar location to the Forest Service; the Service eventually made an offer of $174,000—a figure at least $6,000 less than the one that the owner had in mind. He subsequently listed the property, subdivided into eight lots priced from $20,000 to $181,000, with a real estate agent. No new buildings have been added to the flat at this time.

Mr. Cox donated a portion of his uncle's effects to the Idaho Historical Society, and in December, 1980, two National Guard helicopters flew to the bar with state and guard personnel, as well as Bob Auth, a close friend of Hart's. The men loaded approximately one-thousand items, including clothing, blacksmith tools, guns, knives, bowls, books, and animal skulls, aboard the helicopter and flew the materials to Boise for the state collection. Some of the objects will be part of a permanent exhibit at the museum.

In addition, Rodney and Chana Cox donated a handsome sample of Hart's handcraft to St. Gertrude's Museum at Cottonwood, Idaho, in memory of their son, Jeremiah. The pieces on display include a remarkable percussion rifle, a sheephorn powder horn, knives, a sword, carved wooden spoons, bowls, and boxes, and examples of his metalwork.

The reader/visitor will also notice that since Harold Peterson wrote, most of the towns that he mentions have changed: the population of Boise exceeds 120,000; developers have converted McCall into a condensed variation of Tahoe City; Dixie has become a site for summer homes; and the Forest Service has managed to pave the road to Burgdorf, despite tenacious local opposition.

Changes along the Salmon River, if less noticeable, are also significant: many of Hart's cronies have cached their traps; raft and power-boat traffic has burgeoned; campsites are more calloused; five new lodges stand in places once lodgeless; the Idaho Primitive Area has been subsumed by the River of No Return Wilderness.

Other matters, however, abide: the road to Mackay Bar is still rough enough to churn butter; Hart's cabin, his bombshelter, even his walkway toenailed to the canyon wall remain; tracks of cougar, elk, and mountain sheep still smudge the trails, and the sky above the canyon has kept its clarity.

While the clock has stopped for Sylvan Hart, his story seems no less hardy than the burdock and mountain mahogany that encroach upon his grave, and though Five Mile Bar may be silent, his memory still vibrates there, as softly persistent as the sound of the river. Those who knew him cannot pass the spot without a stir of sentiment.

Cort Conley
Idaho, 1983

The Last of the
Mountain Men

◄◄ ◄◄ 1

O N THE RIVER of No Return, in the country whose name, according to legend, is Light on the Mountains, there lives a gray-bearded man who has turned back time. At Five Mile Bar, beyond which no human soul dwells, Jedediah Smith and Christopher Carson have but recently passed by, and the year is 1844 forever.

As a young man, dismayed by the destruction of the final frontiers, Sylvan Hart recanted civilization and marched off into this Idaho fastness armed with a few staples, an ax, a rifle, and a master's degree in engineering. There, in the last wilderness, where one winter's snows might fall into another's before a visitor came, he became the last of the Mountain Men. Soon to be known as Buckskin Bill, he fashioned his own clothes of deerskin. He constructed adobe-covered buildings with hand-hewn timbers. He mined copper, smelted it, refined it, and made utensils. He even made his own flintlock rifles, boring them on an ingenious handmade machine, to "save the bother of store-bought ammunition." To pay for infrequent trips to Burgdorf (pop. 6, in winter 0), where he purchased only powder, books, and Darjeeling tea, he panned gold.

If this story had been told years ago, it would surely have come to a happy ending. That man, the teller could assert, still lives undisturbed at the confluence of Big Five Mile

Creek and the savage Salmon River. But recently it threatened to have an ironic sequel. Sylvan Hart—for that is really and truly his name—was in danger of being evicted from his chosen wilderness for the very reason that it *was* choice wilderness and the federal government had recognized that it should thus be preserved. As official Wilderness, it was not open to habitation.

The specter of the last heir to Colter and Bridger being driven out by officials conscientiously attempting to guard the remnants of this heritage raised painful questions. Is the pressure of population and progress on the little remaining wilderness so great, one was forced to ask, that wilderness must now be treated as a museum exhibit, to be looked at and admired but not lived in? The sorry answer is "yes." Does this mean, then, that those of us who have occasionally fantasied living as Hart lives are denied any underlying reality to our imaginings? That would be a wretched admission indeed for a nation whose character still depends in no small part on the myth that a man might live thus if he chose. Not least distressed by the prospect of killing so deep-rooted a symbol was the Forest Service itself, which ultimately conceded that one individual living as an authentic frontiersman deserved to continue as a kind of museum piece in himself.

To see what had been saved, I, a young American three generations removed from the frontier, first traveled the great river to Five Mile Bar on the second day of June in the year 1966, hoping to find the myth of total self-sufficience not yet entirely obsolete. I found, in short, that much of what I had been told was incorrect, and that the reality far exceeded any fiction.

For the trip did indeed lead into remote territory. Idaho, firstly, has at least one county—bigger than six states—whose largest town is a ghost town. Boise, its largest city at 72,000, is 145 miles from the Salmon but the nearest reasonably complete outfitting point. McCall (population 1,440), fifty miles distant by air and 150 by land, is the nearest town of any pretensions, and it is a hard eight-hours' drive from the end-of-road closest to Hart's fastness. Packing in means a two-day-long walk over twenty-odd miles of trail from the mostly ghostly gold mining town of Warren, nearly deserted but for one general store.

That route would have been my preference, but I was assured that the river was high enough to render the south-side path dangerous and to prevent Hart from paddling across to ferry me from the better north-bank trail. By river it had to be, so there was still time to speculate about what might be ahead. Somehow I kept thinking of the story I had heard of Johnny-Behind-the-Rocks, an early Idaho recluse noted for having never bathed or removed an article of clothing: his infrequent new garments were put on over the old ones. Named for standing off a whole troop of Indians at his cave door in the Nez Percé War of '77, Johnny died in a hospital in 1935 from the shock of receiving his first bath.

My flat-bottomed aluminum boat jolted over the last rapid and rounded the last bend in the river chasm, whereupon a strangely tropical-looking compound swung into view. As the boat drifted around in the swift current, a long-bearded, helmeted, bespectacled figure appeared on the white-sand beach. It laughed the uproarious, raucous laughter of the mountaineer, doubling over in its mirth and slapping its knees. "Ha! Aha!" snorted Sylvan Hart, and his voice sounded rusty, as if from disuse. Although I thought that Sylvan had been informed of my coming, I later learned it was a total surprise. The spontaneous, unquestioning warmth of his welcome was simply part of his nature.

The boat had not been beached twenty seconds in front of Sylvan's water's-edge home before Hart had begun firing up a huge, ornate copper samovar with a two-foot-high chimney, had explained that samovar meant "self boiler" in Russian (as opposed to samoya, he added, "which denotes either 'dog' or 'Russian savage' and means 'self eater'—the

15

Vistula River natives eat humans, that's why they're self eaters"), and had launched from that into a dissertation on the civilizing influence of the fur trade in Russia.

The samovar was so remarkably crafted I did not realize until much later that Hart had made it. I did, however, comment on the copper squirrels scurrying over its top. Hart seized upon the opportunity to observe that they were gray squirrels, who can dodge flintlock rifle fire, and that their eyes were beads made in India by some eleventh-century process: "The design was later copied by a Frenchman who got an Indian dagger in the kidney for his trouble."

Scarcely had the juniper-wood fuel started boiling the tea water when Hart leapt up again. "I must show you my football uniform," he said, bounding into his kitchen house. "They tried to get me to play on the scrub team upriver. They pretended to be Vandals—that's just another breed of Goth—but they don't have the right uniforms." (Note: the University of Idaho, many miles down the river, calls its teams the Vandals.) Hart emerged dressed in bearskin shorts, bearskin jerkin, horned-copper helmet, brass boar medallion on a shiny brass chain, and brandishing a fearsome brass-handled sword. "I'll be captain," he said, "we'll beat the varsity, and I'd like you to take some pictures to send to my little relations. They've never seen me."

A first sample of Buckskin Bill humor, the uniform had been fabricated by Hart almost solely for his own amusement. (The pants, however, do have one practical use; known to his friends as "Buckskin's bikini," they make a stool unnecessary when fishing on the ice.) It was nowhere near the last. A further example is the "love letter" Buckskin sent one-time visitor Miss Idaho, all in Indian pictographs and painted on the shoulder blade of an elk. Miss Idaho presumably kept that *billet* in her hope chest, but Hart retains another such letter, this one illustrating Washington's capture of Trenton from the drunken Hessians.

Amidst this assault on my credulity, Sylvan interjected a

story to the effect that not long before my arrival a mountain lion had killed and buried a doe just outside his garden gate, returning two nights to finish off the deer. "There we were, the two of us," Hart said. "I was out there to guard my garden, the cougar was lying just outside to guard his kill." This was no joke. He could easily point out a fresh round cougar pawprint, the remnants of the unfortunate victim, the brush the cat had pawed over it, and the depression where the lion had bedded down to keep an eye on deer and Hart. "Lots of people live a whole lifetime," as Sylvan observed, "without having a mountain lion in their garden.

"A cougar once made a kill on that little bench over there, too," Sylvan said, pointing. "I heard coyotes howling up there and went to investigate. It was an elk, and I figured they couldn't have gotten an elk by themselves. And then I found leaves scraped up over the carcass, which proved it was a lion kill."

Fact is hard to separate from fancy on Five Mile Bar; the facts tend to be so fancy. The elk-antler door handles would be a good case in point except that there are so many others. It is difficult to believe, looking around the compound, that practically every ingenious element of its orderly clutter was fashioned by Hart's hand. The degree to which everything is made and placed for some specific purpose is nearer yet to incredible. Even the pastel red of the buildings, achieved by mixing lime into the homemade plaster ("The lime oxidizes the ferrous limonite to ferric hematite," he explains), is designed to harmonize with the complementary pastel greens of surrounding apple and apricot trees.

The effect enhances an already esthetic, if rampantly eclectic, architecture. Kitchen house and blacksmith shop, linked in a Tennessee dogtrot pattern, are in turn joined to the two-storied, balconied living quarters by an open South Seas roof house. Those living quarters, by the way, demand further mention. The lower room, masoned of native stone for warmth and because the stone was already there, serves

17

as winter quarters. The frame upper floor, Buckskin's summer house, boasts a bay window—a B-18 plexiglass cockpit canopy Billy packed in on his back. In the balcony, there's a fine place to sleep in fair weather and good protection for firewood in foul. Over all whips and cracks a picturesquely indomitable forty-eight-star flag, its fabric far faded by sun and frayed by wind. "Oh, I'm patriotic," says Buckskin. "Ever' time a bald eagle flies by, I take off my hat."

Of furnishings within the compound, only two are partial ringers: the rocking chair came around Cape Horn in the gold rush, and the table is made from the oak flooring of a building at the ghost town of Dixie. Otherwise, even the pole-picket fence enclosing the 200 by 100-foot plot is an indigenous part of the design. Occasional pickets are much higher than the others, creating an artfully irregular effect merely as a by-product of a scheme to spook deer. "Deer look up at those tall pickets, think the whole fence is that high and decide they can't jump it." Hart explains. The gates, which swing on marble ball bearings, are mounted with bells, not so much to sound pretty as to prevent bears from raiding the garden. "One time a bear knocked down a gate," he went on, "came in, packed out a sheep foot I was pickling in sulfuric acid, and ate it."

Buckskin enjoyed imagining the bear's discomfiture. "Hee, hee, hee," he chuckled, wriggling in his chair. This is a characteristic expression of amusement, just as stroking his beard to a point is an expression of reflective thought. The beard is a beauty, being red at the sides, white at the chin, and straw-colored at the tip. Nothing, in fact, is uncolorful about Sylvan Ambrose Hart, this one-sixteenth-Apache black Englishman born in Indian Territory in 1906, the year before it became Oklahoma. His birthplace, a town named Stone, has vanished without trace. No less distinctive is the nasal, reedy accent, smacking strongly of Arkansas with its conversion of o's into broad a's (sparrah, arrah). Not the least surprising is the vocabulary, ranging from pure dialect to fluent use of words like "syndrome," when talking about the Russian economy, for example.

I was not given much longer to observe Hart in such repose, only his shrewd gray eyes active in the Robert Frost face. He soon bounded up again, sure that I wanted to see his stock of sporting goods. "This here is my skis," he said, having herded me to a storeroom at the customary trot. "I discovered birch was best for slipperiness and hog hide was best to keep from sliding backward on hills. A Norwegian friend told me the same." Buckskin also had homemade bows, "arrahs," crossbows, pack frames, intricate wicker fishing creels, fly rods, and highly crafted snowshoes, but his interest skipped to his boats: "This is my canoe—look how the frame is just like a person's skeleton—and I may make a kayak out of that elk hide over there." We then loped out to the beach, where I was to survey his rowboat, whose name, XAPON, is emblazoned on its prow, after Charon, the dread boatman who ferried dead souls across the River Styx. On the River of No Return, the symbolism was all too apparent.

Of almost equal antiquity is one of Hart's prize enthusiasms, an ancient cave once inhabited by red men long since vanished. "See that soot on the cave roof?" he asked after we had scrambled the few hundred feet to prehistory. "It's so old you can't possibly rub it off." I tried. You can't.

"There are two feet of kitchen midden here," said Hart, pointing to a deep fire hole. "The first thayng we want to know is how old it is. We reach in here . . ." Sylvan did so, pulling out a handful of beach sand and charcoal. "I sent this to be carbon dated, and it goes back to 226 B.C. The half life of the carbon is gone. Think of it. The Great Wall of China was being built, Hannibal was a great man." While Sylvan continued on, telling me why Carthage never amounted to more than it did (primarily, it seemed to him, because it practiced human sacrifice), I looked around the little cavern in awe. Millennia-old bits of smashed bone, heating rocks, mussel shells—it lacked only the hairy, stoop-shouldered householders.

Hart jarred me back into 1966. "Let's look at the bomb shelter," he said cheerfully. "We might be attacked and you wouldn't know where to go." Sure enough, nearer his houses he had blasted, bit by bit, an underground shelter out of solid rock. Sylvan smiled, looking up and down the empty Salmon River, as he said that he, unlike some others, would allow all his neighbors to use his shelter.

The two caves characterize Hart, a man living in several centuries simultaneously, an unassayable amalgam of romanticism, risibility, and realism. "I'm a pretty fierce man for culture," he was saying now. "When I go into some place outside, like a roadside restaurant, I'm likely to ask the waitress, 'Is there any culture in these here parts?' 'Culture?' they say, getting all nervous and stammering. 'Culture? Why no, I guess there isn't any.' "

"Like some lunch?" Buckskin suddenly asked, apparently deciding that I had had as much edification as any man could stand between meals. "Better take it. Here among the savages, you never know when you might get fed." He produced a waxy cheesecloth bag containing what he identified as "a putty of beef tallow." "Put it into hot water and it's ready to eat," he prescribed. "Add some rum, sugar, treacle, anything. Got to have concentrated food."

This was not to be our lunch, it developed. In lieu of rum-laced beef tallow, a potent mince pie served as our concentrated nourishment. Principal ingredients were whiskey, plum preserves, raisins, dried apples, treacle, and gamy meat. One did not expect the pie to emit a low ursine growl, really, but one did rather anticipate coming across a bear claw.

"The crust is very good," I said. "Like it?" beamed Sylvan. "I make it with special pastry flour and bear grease. Bear grease doesn't have the objectionable qualities of any other grease."

After showing me the champagne bottle he uses as a rolling pin, Sylvan trotted me into the kitchen house to see his collection of bottled bear grease and bear cracklings, not to mention apple butter, eggs-and-beets, and canned elk. He said he generally got "twenty-five pounds of grease per bear."

That's a lot of grease, and Hart usually settles for shooting one bear every two years. Alternate years he takes one elk. "Meat from that one animal lasts me pr' near to June," he says. " 'Course, I smoke most of it."

In the case of a bear, Sylvan will gut and skin the carcass, laying the hide aside to be tanned. Next he cuts off the fat, renders it in a huge Dutch oven outside, and seals it up in jars. Then he rubs smoke salt over the meat—perhaps two hundred pounds in all—and, after a couple of days, hooks it into the smokehole back of his fireplace. "I eat the heart right away," he notes, "and a little of the kidney, but not too much. It's rich enough in vitamin A to kill you."

Using salmon flies, hand line, and bullets for sinkers in his teeming, unfished streams, Buckskin catches whitefish, steelhead, bull trout, cutthroat, and rainbows, which he has fresh or smokes, and bakes and eats with goat cheese and tea. If he doesn't catch his first fish within a minute or two, he quits for the day.

"And I buy one or two salt cod a year for iodine," he adds. "The trouble with this water is that it's too clean. No minerals. All the old mountaineers had goiter. The beard concealed that. Same way in Switzerland. One group of Swiss live so far back up in the mountains they still speak Latin. There, if you don't speak Latin or have a goiter, you're a barbarian."

Grouse, fool hens, and snowshoe rabbits, besides some imported beef, supplement Bill's larder. Even a couple of mountain lions have got themselves eaten. "The meat tastes like turkey," Bill claims, "and of course it's light. Animals that eat other animals always have light meat. Animals that eat grass have dark meat." And occasional wildcats or lynxes —"we get them big as deer around here"—bent on raiding the chicken coop find their way, indirectly, into Bill's diet. He shoots them, grinds them up, and feeds them to his banties, which have developed a terrible bloodlust for fresh meat.

One of the mountain lions, also indirectly, still helps keep Buckskin's pantry stocked. Five Mile Bar is relatively frequently visited in the summer these days, and some visitors are rather too expectant of being fed. Now Buckskin is much too polite a man to refuse anyone, but even hospitality has its recourses. "Do you like pickles?" he sometimes asks. "Oh, yes," the visitors chorus. Out comes a jar containing six pickled cougar embryos. "The 58th Variety," Bill says. Buck acquired the embryos the summer he worked for the Forest Service during an emergency. Every once in a while he would leave his post and tend to the pickling operation. "I'd tell the ranger I had to go down and put water on my cougars," he says. "They never *could* get that straight.

"Poor she-lion," Hart explained. "I got it right between the eyes, not realizing it was carrying young ones." He looked regretful. " 'Course, a mother cougar loses a lot of young ones training 'em, anyway. She'll think they can take an old bull elk and it won't be as weak as she thought.

"I *never* kill an animal around my place. I go out and kill a strange animal," he said, adding quickly, "Generally, an animal hanging around down here isn't fat anyhow."

Like any hunter, Sylvan has certain strong views on hunting and game laws. Buck laws, for example, which outlaw the killing of females, make discriminating poaching positively laudable. "You have to kill equal numbers of the sexes. Otherwise the remaining bucks can't keep up with their job and you have fawns coming at all times of the year, in snow and in miserable summer heat." And, although Hart himself has had the slightly unsettling experience of discovering that a mountain lion he was tracking had circled around to stalk *him,* he finds cougars a trifle tame for his taste. "A country like this ought to have something like Siberian tiger to keep hunters from going to sleep on the trails," he suggests. "Besides, elk need something to stir them up, force 'em to use all of their range."

2

ABSENCE OF TIGERSKINS notwithstanding, Buckskin began showing me his home-shot and home-sewn, but not homespun, wardrobe, and I snapped back to attention. "Textiles are no good," he was saying. "A woman could spin and knit all day without keeping her family in socks. But bearskin clothing wouldn't be wearing out just ever' little while." That seemed reasonable, so I nodded.

"It takes a couple of weeks' time to cut and sew a suit of buckskin," Buckskin resumed, "but you see this? This is my first buckskin jacket. Thirty years old and it's good as new." Indeed it was better: the buckskin was worn smooth as velvet.

"Now, what is there about buckskin you couldn't get better on Park Avenue or Bond Street?" Sylvan continued, laying out a newer jacket for inspection, bullet holes in the leather neatly mended. "Just this: a cold wind is what kills you in the mountains, but it can't cut through a big stag hide. ['I am afraid of one thing,' Hart had said once. 'A cold wind. That'll kill you for nothing. You'll just die like a damn fool.'] And buckskin protects you from thorns. Know what those fringes are for? Not for decoration. They let water run off faster, and they make you a poorer target by breaking up the outline.

"One thing about buckskin, though: if you've got a legal

skin, you're in trouble. An illegal skin is homogeneous and thick all over; one killed during the hunting season has prominent veins—necessary to support all that hair—and veins are the first place the leather will crack."

After demonstrating the use of flint and steel and a thong found in the pockets, Bill turned to the trousers. "The great mistake in making pants," he said, "is putting the seam on the inside of the leg. If it gets wet when you have to walk somewhere, it can take the skin right off." Next came mukluks and moccasins, and shoemaking tools. "If you need a moccasin real quick," he advised, "get yourself a fresh elk or moose, cut off its heel and tie the toe."

What Hart actually does when he has a fresh elk, or whatever, is to scrape off fascia from the inside of the hide with fleshing knives and then marinate it in salt and sulfuric acid. "The sodium hyposulfite and hypochlorite get rid of the gelatin in the leather," he explains. When Hart wants colored leather, he uses older methods of tanning. Chopped fine and boiled, sumac makes red leather, alder bark black, mahogany brown. Coffee grounds provide another color, and ashes give white.

Besides the bearhide helmets he wears in summer and bearskin hats in winter (a coonskin cap serves between seasons), Buckskin owns an equally magnificent coat. The back is bear and beaver, the front wolf and badger. This enables him to switch caste merely by facing a different direction, he says. In past times, bear and beaver were noble furs, while wolf and badger were for serfs. The calfskin over the shoulders is there to turn water. One sleeve is skunk, and two pheasant hides adorn the whole. When Buckskin volunteered for World War II, the coat went with him. He became a Norden bombsight technician, equipped with his own workshop by the Army, which apparently thought him a mad genius. Sylvan has no particular love for bombs but, as he said, "It was either that or mop barracks."

The military couldn't have been any more surprised by Sylvan than the Idaho state income tax office, which made the colossal mistake of sending Hart a whole series of letters saying he hadn't paid his taxes. Buckskin finally got dressed in his best stagskins and coonskin cap, took along a rifle and ample supply of provisions, and presented himself at the tax office. "I surrender," he told the slack-jawed bureaucrats. They sent him home and promised fervently never to bother him again.

"Now bedding," Bill announced. "Here's an elk hide I tanned. That's as good for sleeping as anything. It's warm, the hair is hollow so you can stand to have it against you, and it doesn't absorb moisture."

Finally, he displayed his "jewelry," a collection of cut turquoise, agate, and jade, and silver watch chains dominated by a fearful claw necklace. Interspersed among claws from bear, mountain lion, wolves, and the like are sea lion teeth, boar tusks, elk and otter teeth. "If you're an Indian and don't have one of these, you might as well be dead," Sylvan says proudly. An Apache once offered to trade a squaw for it.

The guns with which Buckskin bags his trophies, trinkets, and trousers have aroused considerably more avarice than that. One handmade flintlock rifle, a particularly enviable product of loving craftsmanship, so excited a wealthy Los Angeles businessman that he offered $500 for it. "It's not for sale," Bill told him. The rich Angeleno thought a moment, offered $750. "It's not for sale," Bill repeated firmly. By this time, the man, used to having his money count, was sorely vexed. "$1,000," he snapped. "It's not worth it, but I want that rifle." "It's not for sale," Bill said, as calmly as before. The Angeleno left in a terrible temper. A week later he was back with a blank check. "Fill it out for whatever you want," he barked. "It's not for sale," said Bill. "Damn it," said the man. "You need the money. You *do* use money, don't you?" "No," said Bill. "Not where I live."

The rifle in question has a beautifully hand-bored, hand-rifled barrel, a mechanism with double cock and double-set trigger, and an ornately carved mountain mahogany stock.

Bored to .45 caliber, the barrel is Swedish jackhammer carbon steel, which he had sent in to him.

Although accurately described by Buckskin as "a rotating helix driven by fingers on a headblock nailed to a table top," the machine used to make that rifle scarcely seems sophisticated enough to uncork a pop gun. As for the handmade "rifling saw" which cuts the actual groove, that looks like nothing so much as a half-inch-long bit of scrap metal. Yet if Sylvan, looking down the barrel, can find a flaw, no one else can, and the rifle shoots with deadly accuracy. "It's nothing but muscle power," Sylvan says, "but I really lay into it. That cutter comes out of there smoking."

With its light, steady touch, the firing mechanism is no less astonishing. "The interesting part is a pitiful little thing called a detent," Sylvan explains, taking a listener's comprehension for granted. "It causes the sear to ride over the half-cock notch in the tumbler."

Smoother than rosewood, the stock was simply blackened with sulfuric acid and rubbed to its lustrous deep brown finish by rubbing with the palm of the hand. Its carvings variously depict an old mountain sheep resting its heavy horns on the ground while drinking, two rams fighting, and the exact defensive deployment of a band of bighorns being attacked by eagles.

"I just make one as I need it, but I don't like to spend less'n a year making a rifle," Hart said, opening the patch button in the stock to show the orange flicker feathers inside. They are used to flick dust and lint out of the mechanism.

With deep but understated pride, Sylvan demonstrated how neatly the flint-tipped hammer would shave a sliver of steel off the frizzen, dropping it white-hot into a grain-of-wheat-sized charge of priming powder, and how the firing pan sloped just right to send the resulting fire into the main charge.

The red-striped ramrod is hickory specially cut in East Texas, and even the bright red and green tassels on the accompanying pouch have a specific, if whimsical, purpose. "They might just be decorations," says Buckskin, in one of his frequent indulgences of a taste for melodrama, "or you could tie one to a bush and a pursuer would have to fetch up to study on it."

For more ordinary purposes, the pouch is well equipped indeed. Primer horns, powder horns, bosers, borers, and cleaners, extra flints, rigs to cut flints, vent pickers and scrapers, and even a bullet mold pour out of it in spendid profusion. Sylvan demonstrated the efficacy of one flint cutter on a piece of hard obsidian. "Any doubt in your mind I could skin an elk with that?" he trumpeted. There was no doubt.

Following his regular ritual, Hart showed how he poured powder down the muzzle (fifty grains), pushed in a bullet on a patch cut from a World War I bandage, and tamped it down a bit with three different bosers. After ramrodding the patch down to the powder, he tapped the rod lightly "to seat the bullet" and primed the firing pan. One could still see the shiny spot on the spherical lead bullet where the sprue had been filed off. "Oh, yes, I make my own bullets," Sylvan said. "That's simple, but I do make my own bullet molds, too."

After digressing to apologize for not also concocting his own powder, he resumed, "Now I want to give you a little argument about loading a gun. You have to hand-load a cartridge anyway; might as well be loading directly into a flintlock. If you have to reload quickly, you can always carry bullets in your mouth and papers or pouches of premeasured charge in your hand."

It is not as if Buckskin had only a couple of these cannons. "No mountaineer is worth anything unless he has at least fifteen guns in the house," he says. "Let me show you what you need for tiger." This implement of destruction is a 64-caliber, 14-rifled weapon with percussion cap using a canvas patch and up to ninety grains of powder. An even handsomer pistol with engravings picturing an old bighorn ram digging out feed for young ones actually sees more use, but the .64 would be very nice in case of an elephant stampede.

Some of Bill's other half-breed weapons are equally pretty, equally lethal. One is a 54-caliber rifle with a Hawken barrel picked up off a street in deserted Dixie and a stock salvaged from a British musket bought for a dollar and a half. That Hawken barrel is sawed short to be used on horseback, which means that it probably belonged to an Indian. Another is built around a Remington Hepburn stock attached to a 50-caliber machine gun barrel. The end products do not suffer by comparison with another piece in Hart's collection, a Remington .45 with Plains-type stock brought back from the Battle of Gettysburg by one of his ancestors.

The Remington had originally belonged to a Tuck (one branch of Hart's ancestors) and was brought home to his family by Jim Burke, another relative. Five of the seven boys in that one family of Tucks were killed in the Civil War, and Burke himself later starved to death on Johnson's Island, the notorious Confederate prison camp. It was the Tucks, however, who either had the worst luck or were in the thickest of the fights. In the Revolution, forefather Ned Tuck started the family off by "getting a seventy-five millimeter bullet through the center of the chest at the Battle of Guilford Courthouse," according to Sylvan.

Accompanying this arsenal is a stock of powder and bullets sufficient to fight an Indian war. In event of demand exhausting even this supply (one box of cartridges is labeled, enigmatically, "For World War III"), Buckskin could turn to his knives.

Most formidable of these are a matched set of three of the most enormous Bowie knives, their guillotine-like blades inscribed with mottoes such as "Liberty or Death," "Kill or Be Killed," and "Nuts." The most massive, modeled directly after one given to Daniel Webster by Sam Houston,

28

confirms Sylvan's description: "A Bowie knife like that is nothing but a small sword.

"There are only half-a-dozen really good knife patterns in the world" by Hart's count, and he has made samples of each. Besides the Bowies there are classic daggers "originally used" as he describes them, "to drain sinovial fluid from fresh-killed animals—that's what spoils the meat"— Indian crooked knives, Arabian daggers, French knives, which Sylvan uses to chop and to filet, and one surgical knife "modeled after one I saw in a Brueghel painting." "But if I had to have only one knife, I'd take this nine-inch Bowie," he concluded, fondling its mountain sheep-horn handle, the sheep's blood forming a red pattern in the tang.

The tools with which the man creates these masterworks and others are a cornucopia of finely tempered, ingeniously crafted instruments—hundreds of them—too specialized and original to have names. There are tools for scraping inside horn, tools for cutting inside small holes, tubular tools for carving inside rifle channels, tools for checkering gunstocks, tools for putting grooves in skis, tools to shave steel, tools like hunks of super-coarse file. There are also scrapers, gouges, skewed chisels, awls, auzes, and fine-tolerance dies, taps, and punches in sizes and shapes beyond counting.

Behind a shopdoor whose hand-lettered sign advertises "Blacksmithing and Millinery" lie more handmade steel-working tools (the ubiquitous bear grease is used to temper steel without cracking it), copper-working tools, silver-working tools, wood-working tools and, of course, blacksmithing tools. "Hardly anybody has a really complete set of blacksmith tools anymore," says Sylvan, "but I do: a hardy, a flatter, all of them." Hardly anybody has a forge made from an old Sibley army stove either, but Sylvan does, and he salvaged the stove from an abandoned moonshine manufactory up Grizzly Gulch.

That still never was a paying proposition, but it did succeed in providing basic materials for much of Hart's copperware. Most of the rest is copperplate used in mining, and it still had gold amalgam sticking to it.

"My idea of art is to make sure you have good utensils, things you use every day, before you go fooling with pictures," Hart declares. "That's the Scandinavian idea, too." No Danish artisan should object to the comparison. Hart's lowliest pot is worth seeing. Bowls, ladles, kettles, lanterns, candleholders, samovar, coffeepots, tea balls, griddles, and skillets all bear the imprint of Hart's original feeling for design. Using his special set of long-nosed tools to work inside the utensils, he heats the copper to red heat, immerses it in water—"that softens it, whereas it would harden steel"—and beats it out, the metal curling and flowing under the hammer, until he has artifacts that have excited certain Idaho museum curators even more than his guns.

The copperware is also uniquely utilitarian, as I soon had chance to discover. After a long day of examining life far from the blessings of civilization, it was nearly time to have dinner. First, however, a batch of sourdough needed making, and that demands at least overnight aging. "Every place has some food that is positively rotten and is positive that you'd like to have some of it," Sylvan warned. "In this country we have rotten sourdough."

Rapidly assimilated into an appetizing bowlful, Hart's confection of buckwheat, corn meal ("I grind m'own"), turkey red wheat flour, sourdough ("great fights have been fought over whether this is a yeast") and New Orleans molasses ("the sugar makes yeast work faster") laid to rest any worries about the next day's hungers.

Thought having been taken for the morrow's needs, we strolled around Sylvan's garden seeking what we might devour. Even in earliest summer, the choice was impressive. At various stations in the 10,000-square-foot plot—fertilized by, among other things, one buried deer, two bear heads, and one cougar skeleton—sprouted asparagus, parsnips, carrots, beets, cabbage, corn, squash, cucumbers, cantaloupes, peppers, garlic, strawberries, horseradish, rhubarb, rutabaga ("thirty-eight chromosomes, eighteen of them cabbage and twenty turnip"), kohlrabi, kidney beans, purple beans, white potatoes, purple potatoes. . . .

Purple potatoes? "Just like the Incas used to have," Buckskin explained, cutting one for my inspection. It was indeed a shiny purple. "They taste the way potatoes ought to taste. All cultures have their tasteless staples: rice, poi, and in our case, White Rose potatoes. The only thing that makes *those* taste good is that there's some good-looking young lady serving them to you."

Trees of more ordinarily colored peaches, pears, apples, and apricots ring the garden. "Apricots," says Hart, "are about the best fruit there is. They're nourishing, and you can roast the seeds. The hardiest mountaineers in the world, the Hunza in the Himalayas, press apricot oil. Of course, that whole colony was started by three deserters from Alexander the Great's army, and walking across a thousand miles of desert is good natural selection."

In addition to domesticated flora, there are such in-between species as perpetual onion. "If you see those," Sylvan explains, "you know the Hudson Bay Company has been there. The Company used to give seed, eight pounds of flour and five of salt as board, and its traders had to grow or shoot the rest." Hart also plucks certain wild groceries for his table. Adjacent to the other is an informal garden of Oregon grapes, captain's purse, squaw cabbage, dandelion, shadbush berries, currants, rose hips, gooseberries, oyster plant roots, and broadea roots, which "taste like raw peanuts," Hart claims.

"Or you can take sap from birches and make syrup," Bill says. Army survival school instructors have brought classes to sit at Hart's feet and absorb lessons on self-preservation in the wild. "You've got to take thought as to whether a certain wild food is worth the effort," he tells them. "If you have to run grasshoppers too hard, you'll run off too much fat. And you must kill as large an animal as possible. Six months on rabbit will kill any man."

His guest having consumed a few samples of such exotic fare, Hart restricted the evening's meal to more conventional vegetables. "Do you like asparagus?" he queried. "I don't too much myself—the Emperor Diocletian did—but I'll take some for the soup. Great spring for onions. And beans, of course."

Beans, onions, asparagus, carrots, pieces of imported chuck roast, unidentified bones, and chopped potatoes ended up in a massive kettle of the variety one associates with the parboiling of missionaries. For those who might have wondered, purple potatoes, when boiled, turn a bright blue. "This is really more stew than soup," Sylvan admitted. "We can't honestly talk soup until it has enough gelatin in it to turn solid when it gets cold." Whatever it was, it was delicious, and the colors didn't hurt a bit. Together with the bright green beans and bright orange carrots, the bright blue potatoes deserved immortalization in technicolor.

After some of Bill's preserved pears, we settled comfortably down to talk and to watch a candle wage its unequal struggle against gathering dusk. During a pause, I looked around the kitchen house. Of all the thousand articles, useful and quixotic, that inhabited its pegs and shelves, the boxes and boxes of tea caught my eye. Besides a native variety of tea the Hudson Bay Company once had Indians pick and then sold back to them mixed into the Chinese tea which the redmen bought from the company, I saw tins of mint, Keemun, Lapsang Souchong, South American maté, gunpowder, jasmine, India, Russian, Nung Cha, Japan pan-fired, Irish, Ngun Jun, ginger, Habucha, Woo Long, Dichec's black, Darjeeling, Earl Gray's and English Breakfast teas lined up in ranks and rows. Most of the teas had been sent him as gifts. The prize of the lot, a self-labeled "Boston Harbor Tea, 'Bawstonaba Registered,' Blended and Packed by Davison Newman & C° L^td, 14 Creechurch Lane, London E.C. 3, The Firm which supplied Tea 1773–1774 for the historic Boston Tea Parties," preserved on its backside a complete if microscopic copy of the "Petition of Davison & Newman to King George III claiming compensation for Chests of their Tea thrown into the harbour of Boston, Massachusetts, by Persons disguised as Indians." The petition's language was so aggrieved as to be slightly incoherent, and it had the date wrong by seven months.

"Is it true," I asked, "that you used to go to town for nothing but tea, books, and powder?" "When it's forty miles to town on ropes and snowshoes," said Buckskin dryly, "that's about all you can carry." His total supply of other imported goods, some fifty dollars' worth, was brought in on a neighbor's pack string once a year, in the autumn. Flour, sugar, coffee, oatmeal, rice, and raisins were almost the sole freight. "One year, when I had been prospecting at Florence (another gold ghost town), I walked clear to Grangeville (96 miles from Five Mile) and brought back all my supplies myself," remembered Buckskin. "That wasn't a good winter. But then I spent a number of those first winters without even bacon or potatoes."

Later in my stay, Sylvan was to show where he had lived when newly come to the Salmon, sleeping under a tree and baking in a stone oven. He pointed out a depression that had been a subsequent dugout, remains of a corral and a chickenhouse, and then-recent Indian tepee holes. "The Indians had the same idea I did," he observed. The land was a placer mining claim early in the thirties, and Hart bought fifty acres for one dollar. "You could have bought the whole Salmon River for $10,000," he says.

3

ONE OF Hart's occupations in his early days on the Salmon was frequent long hikes to visit the still-living pioneers of the region, his purpose being to pick their brains for every grain of knowledge of the fading frontier life. Many became the young man's friends, notably Pres Wilson, whose family had traded with Andrew Jackson; John Moore, "an honest moonshiner" who made his likker from apples; and old Henry Smith, discoverer of the richest mine both at Warren and at the fabulous Florence bonanza, who left Buckskin his treasured Haenel rifle. In that remote country, as Sylvan says, "even if someone didn't like you very well he was still kind of glad to see you." In the case of the story of Henry Smith, and also some other tales told by Sylvan, I was later able to trace down further details and bring them back to Hart.

Polly Bemis, famed in legend as a bride won in a poker game, lived just ten miles downriver until 1939. Her real story is perhaps more interesting. Brought to Warren as a Chinese slave girl, she became a dance-hall hostess at the place where miner Frank Bemis was shot in a gunfight. Polly nursed Bemis back to health, and in gratitude he married her.

" 'Course you had to beware of those who might paint the lily white," Buckskin said. "There was a small, bird-beaked

35

black Englishman who may well have been a James like he claimed, but one old guy on Rabbit Creek, a famous old 'prospector', actually cut wood for a donkey engine."

Be that as it may, there were plenty of authentically rough characters left over from the times when there were 1500 men at famed Campbell's Ferry, now silent, hundreds of whom carried about gold dust from the Thunder Mountain boom in quart jars. "Even as late as the forties," says Sylvan, "an oldtimer shot and killed another man around here. His complaint was that the other man packed off his wife and kept her several days at a time. Nothing was ever done about it, even though the older man was also suspected of killing a stepson who just disappeared."

People have always, it seems, had a way of vanishing without trace along the River of No Return. Old man Campbell himself, owner of Campbell's Ferry, walked out his kitchen door one day to bring in firewood and was never seen again. "Easiest country in the world to murder anyone," Hart says comfortably. "Suppose you go back East and marry someone and decide you don't want that kind of woman at all. Just bring her out here on a hunting trip and say she got lost. This is too big a country to search all of it."

The grand finale of one of Idaho's other-worldly sunsets now demanded our attention. It took me two weeks to see what made these sunsets so strangely beautiful: the air is so pellucidly clear that the sundown is never red, not even purple, because there is simply not enough dust to diffract light sufficiently. Instead tints of green, reflected from the dark forests, vary the turquoise, azure, ultramarine, and purest blue of the sky. That latter blue is the poignant blue of Idaho's flowering camas prairies, and in its extraordinary depths one glimpses the very color of a pioneer woman's eyes, the very gingham of her frock.

It was now full night. The candle flame shifted and flickered in a faint draught, rearranging the shadows. Its light now lit what appeared to be three skulls, resting in a recess over the fireplace directly under a muzzle-loading rifle, a buffalo powderhorn, and a bullet mold. The death's heads on the left and right were slit-eyed, fanged cougar skulls; that in the center, reposing on an ancient Greek Bible, looked all too human.

This, it unfolded, was another "lost" Idahan. Hart, who found the relic washed up on the river edge, deduced that its previous owner had been a boy shot for stealing provisions from early settlers, then thrown into the torrent.

"We still have drownings, too," Hart assured me. "Guy not long ago killed nearly his whole family—himself, three children, and the grandmother—when his motor quit in a rapids. Called Lucky McKinnon, he was, because as an Air Force pilot he had been shot down twice over jungle and survived.

"Somebody asked me once if I wanted to row across during high water. 'Don't b'lieve I do,' I said. 'If you fall into that water, you're too likely to die.' It's so cold you don't have time to drown, really. You die of a heart attack."

Some perils are less lethal, of course. Sylvan remembers that a man named Willis was shot at by a man named St. Pierre some time ago. St. Pierre, who claimed Willis and dog had "looked like two black wolves," hit Willis dead center in the barrel of a rifle he had been carrying. Hart still has the barrel, neatly bisected by the bullet. "If you survive something like this, you won't live very long," he said, showing it. "You've used up your chances." Willis died of natural causes shortly after.

Buckskin himself squanders no chances. "If I ever do find a gold mine," says Sylvan, a part-time prospector, "I'll just about have to have a partner. If people know you have a rich claim, someone's too likely to come up and shoot you, like what happened on Middle Fork. Some young guy got an old one, and they never even prosecuted."

I was inclined to discount this as one of Sylvan's occasional dramatizations until someone else told me that a couple of river rats in the region had openly boasted of how they would someday ambush Hart and appropriate all the gold they fondly but erroneously expected he had squirreled away. The implication was that their plan involved liberal use of firearms. They had better bring a lot.

Skippers as well as jumpers abounded. "J. R. Painter, an orphan from Philadelphia, somehow got the Du Ponts to invest $60,000 across the river," Sylvan snickered, gesturing upstream toward the old Painter mine, whose weathered mill still hulks large in the deep canyon. "That wasn't so bad, even if the mine warn't no General Motors, but he also bought a ranch and wrote the check on the Du Ponts. Last I saw of him, he was leaving for Honduras just ahead of the Pinkertons.

"There *is* supposed to be a lost mine up on this mountain, Little Sheepeater," Buckskin pointed. "Supposedly the guy who discovered it built a cabin over the gold-bearing ledge for shelter and to mark the spot. He left, and a forest fire burnt every stick of wood on the mountain to ashes. But then once you start believing in lost mines, you're soon likely to become a lost soul."

Though disdaining such tales, Hart does prospect regularly; just last summer he packed off for a long pickax party. "If you're a prospector you'll prospect," he shrugs. "If you knew a curse was on you so you'd never find anything, you'd still prospect. Around here you can hardly take a pan without getting gold, but it's scattered around too much. Gold is the darnedest stuff. If you get the smallest particle there is, you can still see it, even if it takes a million colors to make a penny's worth. And this Salmon River gold is 900 fine with 1000 being the finest there is."

One suspects, actually, that he goes on these expeditions largely to explore new territory, even if he does grumble, "Anytime you go someplace you think nobody's ever been, you're sure to trip over some woman's shoe." What, after all, would Hart *do* with a bundle of money? "He could speculate with it," suggests his nephew Rodney Cox, a stock analyst. "If he lost the whole wad, he'd be no worse off." Of

38

his scattered relatives, Cox is the one who keeps in closest touch with Sylvan.

"You see some fine things in this country," Buckskin reminisces of his jaunts. "We was up on Horse Heaven last June and I looked down in the canyon and saw a bolt of lightning begin and end below us. Some of those lightning bolts are a foot wide. If they hit a tree, the tree *explodes*. You see that for free. Sometimes ball lightning comes rolling down the hill, rivulets running down from it like molten gold. St. Elmo's fire is common, and I once had some come down the stovepipe while a visitor was making coffee. I heard this screaming and yelling. 'It came right out of the coffeepot,' he said.

"Then there are places down on South Fork where you can find rows of pottery set just as the Indians left them. Lucky McKinnon found a cave with baskets, too. In a good dry cave, those baskets could have set there five hundred years."

Old Indian signs and art, which, self-taught, he has learned to read, also captivate Hart. His favorite story in that regard is of finding an ancient sign up South Fork just as the Idaho skies were preparing to open up and let loose. "At first I thought it was a trail marker," he recalls, "but it was a 'house' sign, meaning hogan, tepee, hotel. There was nothing there but a straight, sheer cliff, but I spread my bedroll for the night anyway. Well, the drip from that pouring rain missed me by just *this* much all night. A message from one thousand to fifteen hundred years ago had kept me dry."

On one stretch away from home, Sylvan actually saw a preparation for a modern, miniature Indian war. The Forest Service, which regularly hires Indians as smoke jumpers and firefighters, made the mistake of putting two historically inimical tribes together. The tribes hadn't seen each other since "pacification" by the white man, but as soon as they met, old hatred flared. "They were actually singing

39

and yelling and dancing around bonfires, ready to attack, until somebody separated them again," Hart says.

A number of Sylvan's earlier trips were made to visit ladies he met while a graduate student at the University of Idaho. I suggested, tentatively, that having had a family might have endangered Hart's freedom to live this life. Women like bright lights and shiny things, and in the case of children school, for example, would be a problem. "Well, yes, but it's not that so much," he said forthrightly. "I just haven't had enough selection, haven't seen enough people to see any I wanted to marry. It's not that I wouldn't.

" 'Course you see how this is the only place on the river with good firewood," he said, changing mood. "That's because there's never been a woman here. A woman sets around the stove all day burning fuel." Besides, Buckskin implies, he doesn't regard too kindly some of the women he does see. "I was taking a little bath in the river one day when I heard all this hollering and screaming," he relates. "I had just had time to get on my long red underwear when these women came round the bend yelling that their rubber boat was leaking. I hauled them out, prob'ly saved their lives, and all the while those frozen-faced women were sitting there looking disapproving. Well, first, I had less hide showing than they did, and then I don't think they were showing any proper appreciation a'tall. I think they thought I wasn't decent. Clothes or no clothes, I'm *always* decent."

Somehow this example of feminine ingratitude cantered off into a discussion of Lewis and Clark, possibly on the premise that if a bunch of crazy women could get down the river, William and Meriwether could, too. Sylvan—he has facts like these at tongue tip—pointed out that the fateful expedition reached and named the River of No Return at high water. In early spring, I supposed, they would have left Mr. Jefferson signing widows' pensions.

"It's interesting to think," Hart ruminated, "that Lewis spent his twenty-ninth birthday crying because he would never amount to anything. And now that we run onto the subject, they should have given Lewis and Clark a medal and then sent them to kindergarten to learn to read and write. At one point their journal describes a grizzly as being 'stonded.' Now does that mean astounded or stunned or drunk or what? That bear's feelings are lost to posterity forever."

It was late, and we prepared for bed at the place Lewis and Clark had not reached. The moon was not yet risen, but starlight poured down into the canyon, turning the granite opposite wall a gravestone white etched with black, black pines. City people forget—or never know—how bright a clear, clean night can be. Where the stars are not shut out by the visual pollution of mercury vapor arcs, the eye can see again. At Five Mile Bar, it can see a dark, mighty river under a pristine sky.

Such purity is rare in a night now, but not at Five Mile Bar, and each evening before settling into my sleeping bag on one of Sylvan Hart's improvised beds I watched the black-green Salmon hurry down to the Snake, watched Sylvan's collection of skulls phosphoresce softly in the half-light.

Two MULE DEER woke first, this and many another morning, and came down to visit the compound. "My best ram watched the boat and, soon as you left, he slipped down," Buckskin was to tell me when I returned from a brief absence several days later. "That blond bear, the one with cubs, was here, too, and a couple of ewes came around." But of course, I thought, mountain sheep, bears, elk, coyotes, wolves, and lions frolic about Buckskinville night and day, except when a friendly, appreciative visitor is present. Bill did, however, have several snapshot closeups grouping half a dozen or more curious bighorns, and I saw myself how it is necessary when flying in to not-far-distant Chamberlain Basin to buzz the landing strip to chase off dozens of sunbathing elk.

Besides a human-loving, feline-hating, rattlesnake-pointing Manx cat and "a most well-behaved snake" living in his chimney, Buckskin has a host of such friends. His "pet toads hop in the house and mop up any insects," "the grouse clean out the strawberries," orioles debug the tomatoes, lowly magpies chase off fruit-eating avians, and hummingbirds simply entertain: "a half-ounce hummingbird defending its home will make an eagle scream, drive him right out of the country," claims Hart. I was incautious enough to ask Buckskin how he spent Christmases. "Way I celebrate Christmas is this," said Bill, pokerfaced. "I've got a rabbit here, and I feed him a handful of carrots.

"Why, these animals are the same as most people, or better," says Sylvan undefensively. "Go down Seventh Avenue in New York and you can see people, but you can't talk to them. You'd be better off seeing animals. Except you could talk to the animals without bothering them."

Hart has time to enjoy these creatures because his is a life stripped of all nonpurposeful work. "I work three, four hours before it gets hot, then *maybe* two more after the sun goes down," says Sylvan. "Or I might just stop and watch otter play. If you lived in a place like this and had to work hard eight hours a day, you'd be a pitiful incompetent."

Time preparing meals Hart does not count, and breakfast, which immediately follows Animal Hour and is often the biggest meal of the day, again demonstrated why: he is too handy at it to consider it work. Moreover, Hart has the help of ingenious gadgets like his "bannack iron," a kind of Bronze Age waffle iron. On this estimable contrivance, generously lubricated with bear grease, he will fry up sourdough pancakes, steaks, and eggs in rapid succession. All approach culinary perfection, which Sylvan attributes to the design of the implement, but the flapjacks, awash in butter and various syrups brewed up from raspberries and melted-down butterscotch or lemon drops, are particularly fine. "It's a pitiful shame you came here when we had least to eat," Buckskin apologized a few days later. We had just consumed a gallon of fresh strawberries flavored with sugar, vanilla, and gentian root.

Weaving slightly under the weight of this Buckskin breakfast, we set out on trips up Five Mile Creek and down the Salmon to Bill's first cabin, but not, however, until the day's water had been fetched. Eschewing the hand-carved yoke he sometimes uses, Buckskin merely grabbed a bucket, then buckled on a pistol, as he always does on even so short a venture.

"That young lion shares my waterhole," he said, trotting

44

out his best country-cousin expression. A more plausible reason is the prevalence of rattlesnakes. "The whole igneous Salmon canyon is just one big crack in a mammoth granite basolith," as Hart says, and rattlers thrive on the warm air seeping up through fissures from deep in the earth. In compensation, mosquitoes, gnats, flies, and vermin of any description are rare or nonexistent. "Only had houseflies the last five years," growls Sylvan. "Someone finally brought us in a few." Even bacteria and viruses languish and die. They certainly find no lodgement in Hart's innards. Sylvan, who drinks little or not at all, gargles daily with Hudson Bay Company rum, the gasoline that won the North. It is 151 proof.

As for outards, says nephew Rodney Cox, "tub baths in winter just started a year ago. Before that he used to run down through the snow and take a bath in the river." No Johnny-Behind-the-Rocks he.

We scooped up water now from tumbling Five Mile just above one of Hart's bridges, a huge adzed tree felled to span the stream exactly where wanted. "Notice the almost imperceptibly thin growth rings around 1886," pointed out Hart. "That was a very, very dry year, the year Teddy Roosevelt went out of the cattle business."

We bushwhacked up the near side of the creek, beating our way through ocean spray, mock orange, wildrose, and trumpet vine, with Sylvan naming in Latin all the species as we passed. This can be intimidating. "Ranunculus bulbosus," he said, gesturing imperiously at one particularly inoffensive little flower. "What's that?" I asked, thinking it looked somehow familiar. "Buttercup," he said.

Buckskin suddenly pounced on a tuft of grass, which seemed, to the untrained eye, no different from any other. But Buckskin had found three bits of white deer hair, elk pellets, and an elk track simultaneously. Progressing, we came upon a whole housing development of small caves formed by a Bunyanesque pile of boulders. "Now look here," Bill directed, "here's a place where lions like to snoop around. See this feather? I saw a coyote get a grouse here, watched him make two neat little piles of feathers as he ate it. Well, a cougar saw those feathers—I saw his tracks —and came back *a year later* to get his own grouse in the same place.

"You should be able to see *that* much hair behind a tree and 'see' a deer," Sylvan elaborated after we had returned to the compound. "You should be able to see an animal for one second and know all about it, what kind it is, what it's doing, whether it's scared or hungry." I complimented him on his knowledge of nature. "Visible nature, yes," Hart specified. "I have trouble taking an interest in anything I can't see. Electrons, that sort of thing, I can't develop any affection for."

After lunch, another bout with Buckskin's muscular mincemeat pie, we trooped off toward Bill's old cabin. On the way out, when I tried unsuccessfully to elicit more philosophy, Sylvan commented that the beans needed one more hoeing. "Thoreau said he did his best thinking while hoeing beans," I observed obliquely.

"Thoreau had a good mind for picking up the subtle changes in things," Hart conceded, "but he lived at Walden only two years. He didn't have the time to really learn his job. A guy like Emerson or Thoreau never did come to grips with reality. He led too sheltered a life. If he had had a cabin surrounded by grizzlies and mountain lions and rabid coyotes and dance hall girls, that would have made a man of him. Westerners have had to survive all that."

Having patched the holes in Henry David's philosophy, we trotted across the log bridge, scampered through some fledgling woods, and fetched up under an Early American Romantic overhanging cliff rearing up a sheer 1000 feet. This cliff, down which boulders, elk, and sure-footed mountain sheep periodically fall, is one reason for Buckskin's bearhide helmets, which are preventatives against a split skull.

Soon, abruptly, the sandy strand below the cliff ended. At

high water, the only way across fifty feet of the swirling Salmon is an hallucinogenic, acrophobic catwalk along the face of the cliff, some thirty feet above the rocks and torrent below. It consists of nothing more than a long series of pine poles lashed end-to-end with wire and a hand cable above to grasp. To construct even this tortuous bridge, Sylvan had to balance on homemade ladders, drill pegs into the sheer rock, stand on those pegs, and drill in more pegs to support the pole walkway. Transversing this engineering marvel is a scary, side-shuffling business relieved only by a currant bush growing out of a crevice halfway across; at least the vertiginous user of the bridge may refresh himself with fresh berries midway. He may need the pause. The catwalk isn't really bad until near the end, where the cable veers outward to the last fastening, necessitating leaning backward while still keeping one's feet on the poling.

"You hear the constant rush of the water and the crunch of the rocks grinding against each other below," says Hart's nephew, who had the pleasure of crossing with a heavy pack when the thing was half under water, "and you think, 'If you happen to slip. . . .' "

This is the trail—there is no other—Cox necessarily took the first time he visited his uncle. Overtaken by darkness, he slept out, somewhat short of the bridge. "Toward the middle of the night, I woke up groggily wondering why I smelled so bad," he says. "Really awfully bad. I finally went back to sleep. Next morning I discovered tracks all around where a bear had circled, sniffed at me, then bedded down a few feet away to look me over."

Between the currant bush and the spot where Cox bedded down is another peril, a rocky slope supposedly serving as a central lodge for the rattlesnakes so abundant in the Salmon country. This was only one of several times we scrambled up and down it, but I never did see any snakes.

A brisk, brief hike brought us to a place purely paradisiacal, a low bench overlooking 180 degrees of river, its breezy

47

greenness of ponderosa and loblolly and high lush grass refreshing the admirable emptiness. "There's 0.2 persons per square mile in this country," said Sylvan, "and that's about right. If you can look out your window and see another house, you're a poor man."

From Hart's former habitation, now little more than a depression, a low pile of stones, and the rusted remains of a stove, one could have seen only a century-old cabin used as a storehouse in pioneer years. Its shredded shakes and long-departed chinking merely reinforced an in-pressing sense of solitude produced by the return to elemental earth of Bill's cabin, one of the region's few human dwellings.

"I've got six months, from November on, when this place is just like it's always been," Hart said, reclining on a grassy slope, sprig of grass between his teeth. "Nobody visits, I get mail twice a month. If I want to go anywhere, I put a pack on my back, get my gun, take off, and stay as little or long as I like. What more could you want?

"For the city man, life is just a jumble, like the facts in a college freshman's notebook. But you can ask me anything about nearly anything, and I can answer because I've had time to think about it."

Every word, every copper pot, had been tacit answer to the basic question, the question I had refrained from asking, but now I wanted it direct. "Why," I said as offhandedly as possible, "did you come here in the first place?" Aware of all romantic speculations as to lost loves and bitter misanthropies, but believing none, I knew too that none of Bill's good friends had ever, in all their talking, gotten Bill's answer.

"It is," said Buckskin slowly but readily, "a custom of my family, going back about three hundred years, for the young men to stay in the woods for at least a year. The first John Hart, who came here in 1635, did it, moving from England to Warhampton in unsettled Bucks County, Pennsylvania. The fourth John Hart, who signed the Declaration of Independence, went to then-wild Staten Island for a while. A succeeding John Hart was one of the first Kansans, and my grandfather went to the Creek country of Oklahoma. I just liked it so well I never came out."

It was quite possible to believe it was as simple and extraordinary as that, a man living as he was just because he liked that life, a descendant of a revolutionary making his own declaration of independence.

If there be those who might think that Sylvan is giving up a good deal in rescinding the twentieth century, his ancestors suffered far greater hardship in order to pursue and precede the frontier, to live the most individualistic, forward, and perilous lives possible in their time. "All thirteen of John Hart's surviving children were lost or scattered during the Revolution," Sylvan volunteers. "He never saw any of them again. Quantrill's bushwhackers stood Grandfather Hart up against a wall in Kansas to shoot him, were scared away, and then looked him up again years later in Indian Territory."

There were many other perils. Hart relatives were burned alive in their house at Farmington, Connecticut, by Tunxis Indians in 1666. The second John Hart was a pioneer settler at Newtown, New York, on the far eastern tip of Long Island. An early Hart was known for having beaten off a large bear with a hatchet, and a Hart woman was reputed to have coolly trapped a houseful of British soldiers, presumably for capture by the Continentals. Over two hundred and fifty Harts are estimated to have fought in the wars of 1776, 1812, and 1865. Embattled farmer Edward, father of the Declaration signer, bravely commanded a regiment, the New Jersey Blues, on the Plains of Abraham in the siege of Quebec, the decisive battle of the French and Indian Wars.

The Hart most touched by history, of course, was the John deeply involved in the Revolution. Honest John, as he was called, was born in the still colonial town of Hopewell, New Jersey, in 1715, the second eldest of three sons and two daughters of Edward Hart and Martha Furman. He grew into a man "tall and straight, with black hair and dark complexion, very prepossessing . . . and very kind," according to contemporary sources. John married pretty Deborah Scudder. First elected to the Colonial Legislature of New Jersey in 1761 and often reelected, "in 1774 he was chosen to the General Congress at Philadelphia, where he was noted for his sound judgment and inflexible determination."

News of Lexington reached Hopewell, New Jersey on a 1775 Sabbath, spread from valley to valley by wildly ringing church bells, by smoking signal fires burning at night, by messengers riding relays of horses. Fiery with indignation, Hart went again to Philadelphia for the climactic events of 1776. Originally sent to the Congress to replace a delegate whose ardor for insurrection was insufficient, Hart was reported by fellow revolutionaries to have "signed the declaration of Independence with particular zeal."

"This man of humble origin, modest and unassuming, without advantages of early education, a plain farmer," as they called him, stood in the highest respect and regard of the learned Franklin, of the patrician Jefferson, and Rush and Adams. When he returned to New Jersey, he was, by acclamation, made Speaker of the nation's first state legislature.

Glory had a somber price. When New Jersey was soon invaded by the British, "the estate of Mr. Hart was devastated and special exertions were made to take him prisoner." The story can be "pieced out" from a number of fragmentary histories, among them *The Genealogical History of Deacon Stephen Hart and His Descendants, 1632–1875.* His classic colonial house pillaged, his property stolen, his sons dispersed, his womenfolk secreted in a log hovel near a grainmill, his health breaking, the graying old man hid in swamps and caves. At first he took refuge in the Sourland Mountains by day and slept in one of his own outbuildings at night, with the family dog as his sole companion. But soon the Hessians hunted him so constantly that he could never sleep twice in the same place. Meanwhile two sons, Edward and Daniel, fought in the Continental Army and one, Jesse, was an officer on Washington's staff.

Christmas of 1776, Washington surprised and routed the Hessians at nearby Trenton. John Hart emerged from defiant exile and reconvened the legislature. How silly for me to have thought at first that Sylvan's elkbone depiction of the Trenton ambush was idle play!

Honest John Hart died in 1779, when the land still echoed with gunfire. History had not yet been turned upside down at Yorktown when his friends buried him on the farm of relative-in-law John Hunt among the children who had preceded him in death, marking his grave with a simple rude stone innocent of inscription. But the alliance with France had been effected and Burgoyne had surrendered at Saratoga. John Hart died knowing that his revolution had won the future.

Hart's descendants "scattered over the south and west," Sylvan's own family settling in Iola in Allen County, Kansas. But somewhere in the family, Buckskin does not know where, are probably still the family Bible, recording births, deaths, and marriages in John Hart's own hand; a deed for the land occupied by Hopewell Church, given by Hart (and the present site of his remains) ; and a piece of John Hancock's table, on which the Declaration was signed. They existed, at least, late in the nineteenth century.

And on a distant river in American territory Honest John could never have known or dreamed, the second most significant Hart lives out his own quiet rebellion. "But I wouldn't want to waste any time in complaining about what currently passes for civilization," Sylvan demurs. "That's too negative. You should be able to see what's wrong about it with just a side glance, that's all.

"The good things a person needs, stubbornness, thinking for himself, don't make him a 'useful member of society.' What makes him 'useful' is to be half dead. On weekends they open all the cemeteries and all those dead people

51

march out. All the same sickly shade of hide, all sunken-eyed, not really seeing anything, just walking about because it's a weekend. Like I say, dead people. Then Monday—well, they don't all go back to the cemetery where they belong. They ought to be honor-bound to go back where they'd be happier, the poor human ciphers lead such pitiful circumscribed lives."

If Hart had his way when the end came, he'd be more alive dead than most of the ambulatory stiffs he disdains. "I'd like to be stuffed and mounted in a museum," he says in characteristic put-on tinged with unquantifiable sobriety. "I'd be wearing my Goth suit, carrying all my guns and knives, and on my forehead would be stamped, 'Be Prepared.'"

Sylvan frequently speaks in these little parables and aphorisms. For instance, he uses the ceaseless battle of millions of his countrymen against billions of dandelions as a symbol of utter uselessness. "Of course, the dandelions nearly always take those lawns," he says. "I'm always glad to see that. A dandelion is a mighty complex thing, and that domesticated grass is an awful silly, moronic kind of plant. It's only right and fitting that the dandelion should win out."

More simply, he said when we were discussing the blood-and-gutless orthodoxy of the unfree, *"The New York Times* is a really good newspaper, particularly for cooking eggs on. The fish oil in its print is so much better for flavor." Or, he says, "a man should have some kind of ideal to pursue. Like independent poverty."

Now, however, Hart turned very serious to say, "My idea of this country and the people who used to be here is that they were better than any other. Besides being courageous and well-educated—Greek, Latin, and all that—they were the most decent people the world ever produced. We won't ever have that again."

Not even implied was his own effort to emulate his predecessors; he had succeeded well, but to have told him that would have been to embarrass him. I said, instead, that all too probably we *would* never see their like again: the absolute freedom and adamant self-discipline that made them were both long vanished. So, very nearly, was their harsh but correspondingly rewarding wilderness.

We talked about how it is the quality of wildness—of some necessary danger or challenge—that is so sorely missed by contemporary young America. To paraphrase Sylvan, it is the need, right, and even duty of young men to get into trouble or at least to flirt with it. If that difficulty, that testing, is natural and directly accessible by simple application of hands and mind, as is a problem of comfort or survival in the wilderness, it stands likely to be more beneficial than synthetic kinds.

Wilderness *does* enhance perspective and refine values. As we walked back to a dinner of superbly cooked steak and fresh strawberries, I thought of Buckskin's remarkable collection of books, everything from *Slow Train through Arkansas* to classics, including *Roughing It* and *Far From the Madding Crowd,* and of how I had commented on a whole subsection comprised of Chekhov, Tolstoy, Babel, Sholokov, Goncharov, Gogol, and nearly everything Dostoevski ever wrote. "You must like Russian literature," I had suggested. "It's not that so much," Hart said. "I'm reading up on slavery and what happens when people are freed. I've concluded that it takes five hundred years to recover and really be free."

The recollection prompted me to ask what he had read most recently.

"*Brave New World,*" Sylvan Hart said.

And what had Buckskin thought of Huxley's chillingly accurate hyperbole of the future? He had liked the Savage, it seemed, because "he was always quoting Shakespeare." "That's about the way it will all turn out," he added as a matter-of-fact afterthought.

I was reminded, as we savored small sweet strawberries obtainable in no city, of the words of the Controller of the brave new World State: "Actual happiness always looks pretty squalid in comparison with the over-compensations for misery." But Sylvan Hart proves that, for yet a little while, you *can* go back again, can abandon the kandy-kolored tangerine-flake streamline world of too many babies.

5

T HE THIRD TIME I was to visit Sylvan Hart, I was determined to reach Five Mile Bar honestly, by Shank's
mare or at least on horseback. After dabbling in the small,
friendly state historical museum at Boise to wash the New
York soot out of my brain, I called Mrs. Don Oberbillig,
who runs the bush radio. Although the date was mid-July,
it seemed prudent to have her radiophone a friend down in
the distant river basin to ask the condition of the long trail
from Warren down to the South Fork of the Salmon. Mrs.
Oberbillig sounded startled by the request. She was quite
positive that the trail, rarely used, was aglop with rotten
snow.

That seemed unnecessarily unpleasant on a trail which
was already a long twenty miles and sufficiently tortuous to
require dawn-to-dark travel under best conditions. A call to
Walt Rubey, a photographer friend of Buckskin from
McCall, seemed advisable. Walt informed me that the previous year, when I had seen central Idaho virtually snowless
by June, had been atypically dry, whereas this last winter
had been more than ordinarily snowy. If I wanted to get
stuck in a snowdrift, the road to Warren from McCall, to
say nothing of the trail from Warren on, was a fine place to
try. Rubey practically guaranteed me rotten snow on the
trail, and the possibility of starting a slide. Then too, he

said, there was the fallen timber tangled all over it, which had discouraged everybody but timberwolves from using the route for quite some time. I said I had looked over the start of the trail the previous year but admitted a bad habit of judging a trail by its beginning. So now it was time to consider the alternative. Although the last 108 miles of the 315-mile route around to Mackay Bar from the north are mostly gravel and uncertain dirt, the trail from there to Five Mile is much shorter and is safely down in the river canyon.

Even the first 107 miles north from Boise, up the tranquil Payette Valley, restore the soul. Horse-mounted cowboys herd stock along the highway. A lonesome crossroads grange advertises square dances each Saturday night. One reaches McCall already in elevated spirits.

Walt Rubey was lobby-sitting at the Shore Lodge on Payette Lake in McCall, his customary spare-time occupation. Above the usual string tie his face, singularly lined and creased by weather, rearranged its contours into a smile as he stood up to shake hands. With the ease characteristic of Westerners both old and new, he was soon relating his stock of local anecdotes where he had left off a year and a month earlier.

I said that mention by Sylvan had interested me in the little-known Thunder Mountain boom of 1897–1907; one of the latest of the gold rushes and the one that came to perhaps the ghostliest end. The district had always been a bit eerie. Thunder Mountain itself had gotten its name from being a perfect sounding board for the crashing lightning of the Salmon River Mountains region. The effect was as if the amplified thunder came out of the depths of the mountains. It scared the Indians, and the white miners were sufficiently impressed to name their district after it, thereby giving the camp one of the most flavorful titles of all. Though it fell into decline soon after 1907, Thunder City once had a newspaper which described it as "bounded on the north by the Aurora Borealis, on the east by the rising sun, on the

56

south by the vernal equinox and on the west by the Day of Judgment."

From Hart, Rubey, and others I had learned that Roosevelt City, once also part of the district, was the town overtaken by the fate of Sodom. Like the wicked city of the Bible, which now lies fathoms deep under the heavy brine of the Dead Sea, it was drowned. Long a decaying ghost, Roosevelt and the whole little valley in which it lay were flooded over when a massive 1909 landslide, unseen by human eyes in the empty remoteness, dammed Monumental Creek, forming a new natural lake. To this day boards, barrels, and pickax handles free themselves from watery graves in the submerged buildings, rise silently through the icy water, and can be found drifting about the surface of the lake by those willing to penetrate to its desolate shores.

Though the Thunder district had more than Lot's unfound ten righteous men, it numbered some bad ones among its inhabitants, too. Walt Rubey's friend, the late Lee Lisenby, 270 pounds without an ounce of fat, as befit a saloonkeeper at Thunder City, remembered a couple of mean characters who used to hang around the premises during his career as barkeep there and pick off a victim now and then. Finally one was slow on the draw. Though it was deep-frozen dead of winter and the deceased had been cordially despised, the bar clientele felt obliged to drag him up the hill and blast a grave in the nearly permafrosted ground with dynamite. Very shortly thereafter, as mixed good and bad fortune would have it, his stubble-faced buddy came to a similar end. Another interment seemed necessary. This time Christian charity went only so far as to spare the departed the common boot-hill practice of caching the stiff in a handy snowbank till the spring thaw. Packing him up the same hill, grumbling all the while, the undertaking volunteers opened the previous hole and dumped the second corpse in on top of the first. Up above Thunder, two remains still share one unmarked grave in skeletal embrace.

My anticipation of seeing Sylvan and his country thus

heightened, I drove thirteen miles west from now tame and touristed McCall to the largely unmodernized wooden town of New Meadows, near the headwaters of the Little Salmon River. Down the street from the empty elaborate brick terminal of an obscure Union Pacific branch line drowses Davenport's Cafe, a refectory surviving the nineteenth century heroically unscathed. While the proprietor and his wife reminisce about Buckskin Bill behind the Davenport's many-windowed false-front exterior, an octagonal Regulator clock ticks minutes with pendular precision. Bountifully frilled hand-sewn aprons invite inspection and purchase in old glass and wooden display cases. Bare bulbs on long cords provide illumination. A stove sits in the center of the floor. Flowers sprig counter and tables, and a delicately antique lady serves the country roast beef. A man arrives with an express package, but his haste is unnecessary, for the passenger train has not run since 1945, and the Northwestern Stage bus is late. On the wall a carved wood sign reads,

> Sweet clean air from east to west
> And room to go and come—
> I loved my fellow man the best
> When he was scattered some.

Down on the Lower Salmon itself, sixty-seven miles north, the old staging town of White Bird anachronistically lines United States federal highway number 95. That highway, spiraling endlessly up the White Bird Grade north of town, is itself a striking symbol of Idaho's saving strength, its disconnectedness. U.S. 95, close to the west border, is the *only* route—road or rail, paved or pebbled—linking north and south Idaho. Nor, in the great primitive areas east of it, is there much coddling of east-west traffic. In the roughly two hundred and ninety road miles between Lolo Pass in the north and a point forty miles south of Sun Valley, there is not one paved road west to Route 95. Thus, when one turns east at county seat Grangeville after passing White Bird Battleground (where the Idaho Nez Percés were defeated in the uprising of '77, bringing Chief Joseph across the river and leading to the historic 1500-mile Long Retreat), the sixty-one miles to Elk City mix a little pavement with a lot of gravel. Beyond that isolated former gold bonanza, the pavement ends and the gravel and grading struggles on only thirteen more miles.

But the enforced leisureliness has its own welcome benefits. As the Elk City road follows the canyon of the South Fork of the Clearwater into the heart of huge, historied Idaho County—bigger than Massachusetts or New Jersey, much bigger than Connecticut, Delaware, and Rhode Island put together—there is time to look up Johns Creek toward Gospel Peak and Umbrella Butte and reflect that up there, at the top of Baboon Gulch, lies what is left of Florence, the once Fabulous Florence of which Sylvan had spoken so often. In 1861 the squeak of saws, the sharp echoing of hammers, the hoarse shouts, and gasps of men bending over gold pans animated that bleak November upland thirty-one crooked miles south. Now nothing remains but a graveyard overgrown with bear grass and wild strawberries, past which only the wind whistles.

"It was not an uncommon thing to see, on entering a cabin," said a contemporary account, "an eight quart pan filled to the brim with gold dust washed out in one or two weeks. All manner of vessels such as oyster cans, yeast boxes, pickle bottles, were in demand in which to store the precious dust." The claim of a prospector named Jacob Weiser yielded $6,600 in a single day, $151.50 in one swirling panful.

Winter started mild that year, it is said, and men poured in. On Christmas Eve, the temperature dropped and the biggest snow ever seen in the northwest began to fall. Eight hundred men were trapped in the Salmon River country. One of the last suppliers to reach camp took ten days for the 125 miles from Pierce and then made it only with the help of the Nez Percés, whose chief, Eagle-from-the-Light, had earlier and angrily warned the encroaching whites to stay off his reserve. By the end of January the only food was flour at two dollars a pound. Men worked in tunnels under ten feet of snow to earn money to live, subsisting for weeks at a time on flour and tea made from tree leaves.

But peril and privation began before the famine and lasted long after. To lessen gunplay over the sluice boxes, it was considered advisable to set up mining laws which read in part, "All dificaltyes Ariseing among the Miners from and after this date Nov. 17th '61 Shall be Settled by the committy elected for that purpose this Committy to act on Millers Creek and tributaries, this Committy to receive $5.00 each for Services to be Paid by the Losing Party. And that this Committy have recourse to the body of the Miners as a means of enforcing their decrees."

I intended to tell Hart about Alonzo Brown, one of the first immigrants, whose excellent *Autobiography* preserves the flavor of Florence. I had found it, left forgotten, in the depths of an Eastern library. Of lesser adversity Brown wrote, "I gave Mr. Watters whom I had known in Roseburg (Ore.) , $20 to pack in my keg of East Boston Syrup. I could have sold it readily for $100 when I got in but I liked it too well myself. With no butter to be had it was mighty good. . . .

"We took two days in going to Florence," Brown recorded. "Camped first night at Little Slate Creek, halfway. There were at least one hundred and fifty men there that night. The Civil War was going on at that time and two of the men got to discussing the war. One was a rebel sympathizer and the other a Union man. They finally got abusive and were about to fight when someone called for men to come out and show their colors. In five minutes we were lined up facing each other, all armed with miners' weapons, pistol, and butcher knife."

Perhaps struck by the farce of a Civil War skirmish deep in the Idaho wilderness, the combatants subsided. Next morning Brown found himself with no complaint worse than that "my heel cords had contracted by climbing steep hills and I could hardly get them to the ground."

After arrival at Florence, Brown bought a crude store for $2500 (it sold for twenty-five dollars in 1863) in which he both worked and bunked. "Men had a habit of getting drunk at the saloons and shooting into stores and tents as they went by. I slept in the store on the floor and to protect myself from the stray bullets fired by drunken men, I piled up a stack of flour as wide as my bed and about four feet high. . . .

"The town was filled with the worst element of the Pacific Coast, and thieves and gamblers from the East. The saloons and gambling houses were wide open night and day and a man was killed nearly every night."

"The year of 1862 was a fearful time," Alonzo's brother Loyal remembered, "full of danger for life and property . . . the most atrocious crimes were committed and no person felt secure, day or night [until finally] Judge John Berry and brother were on their way from Florence to Lewiston with a pack train, when they were robbed on Salmon River by English, Peebles, and Scott. . . ." After the robbers were pursued by Berry to Walla Walla and arrested, "The people, finding no security for life and property and having no regularly established courts, concluded something must be done to suppress crime and took the matter of meting out justice into their own hands." In other words, Scott, English, and Peoples were hanged. All of this, I knew, Hart would listen to with relish.

The extravagantly notorious Plummer gang, always alert to a good thing, also worked the territory. One of the most favored tales of old Florence concerns three Plummer cronies, Henry ("Cherokee Bob") Talbotte, Bill Mayfield, and William Willoughby, and a rather commercialized young woman known only as Cynthia. Hart later told this long, fascinating version of it which I reconstructed afterwards. For it is, without doubt, the area's favorite legend.

Mayfield, a romantic figure of chiaroscuric character, first fell into Plummer's debt when that chivalric outlaw helped him escape prison after he had stabbed Sheriff John Blackburn through the heart in a barroom. A web of conflicting and interlocking stories differ as to whether the stabbing took place in Nevada City, California, or Carson City, Nevada. Little known, perhaps, are the facts that Blackburn was drunk and abusive, that he tried to arrest Mayfield without a warrant, and that he was so unpopular that leading citizens helped dig Mayfield out of the town jail. In any case, Mayfield and Plummer met Talbotte (sometimes called Talbert) in Walla Walla, Washington, and the three went on to Lewiston, Idaho. In each place Plummer, a handsome devil who made rather a hobby of that sort of thing, seduced the wife of a prominent local man. When Plummer tired of Cynthia, he passed her on to Mayfield, and the latter took her to Florence when he, Cherokee Bob and Willoughby removed to that flourishing community.

Shortly Cynthia, who "possessed many charms of person and considerable intelligence [but] had an eye to the main chance, ready to bestow her favors where they would command the most money," according to a marshal of the territory, began to cozy up to Talbotte, particularly since Cherokee Bob was now a successful barkeep, having set up in business by the elegant expedient of throwing out the lawful owner. "On his part Bob made no concealment of his attachment for the woman, and when charged with harboring an intention of appropriating her affections, boldly acknowledged the soft impeachment." The two partners were faced off, ready to draw down on each other, when the gentlemanly Mayfield decided to ask Cynthia her choice. She took Bob, although she loved Bill. Mayfield, as gracefully as chagrin would allow, turned her over to Cherokee Bob, who in respect and regret presented his old friend with a large sum of money before he left town. Cynthia cried hard but let him go.

As Sylvan's account continues, with still further allusions

to various contemporary sources, the scene shifts to next New Year's Eve. Otherwise occupied in helping celebrating miners lighten their pockets, Talbotte deputized Willoughby to escort the comely Cynthia to a ball attended by all the town's most respectable citizens. At the dictate of the more orthodox ladies present, Cynthia and friend were asked to leave. "Scowls and sneers met them at every hand. A general commotion took place among the ladies." Since Willoughby was acting in a relatively disinterested capacity, he left.

Talbotte, a widely traveled gunman with no reputation for a forgiving nature, regarded the social slight less kindly. Next morning, having plentifully fueled their indignation the remainder of the night, Talbotte and Willoughby set out to avenge the affront. Unfortunately for the chivalrous badmen's notion of justice, ball committeeman Jakey Williams's friends, taking offense at the number of bullets fired his way, filled both with a fatal quantity of lead. Willoughby died in the dirt streets of Florence, blood spurting from sixteen wounds. Talbotte lingered three days. His final words were, "Tell my brother I have killed my man and gone on a long hunt." Cherokee Bob's weatherworn wood headboard still stands on cemetery hill, among the nearly one hundred men who died with their boots on in Florence's first two years.

Cynthia rejoined Mayfield in Placerville, a town south and west, in time to see him cut down on Granite Street by a blast from a shotgun. Over Bill's body, she swore a vengeance which never materialized. Instead, she "entered upon that career of promiscuous infamy which is the certain destiny of all women of her class." It was said that Cynthia eventually became the cause of more gunfights and broken friendships than any other woman in the Rocky Mountains.

Yet not sudden death but life—wild, riotous, laughing life—was the mark of a camp like Florence. A man might have to rise before the sun and work in an icy stream, but the tang of the sharp morning air and the shock of the cold, clear water let him know he was alive. And when he could stop working, the smell of pines in declining sunlight and the luminous glow from canvas rooftops excited the sense of Cibola and Quivira, of a mythical city at the outermost frontier of human restlessness and yearning. Heard from hillside or muddy street, the click of ivory chips on hard wooden tables was as much music to the miners as the merry sawing of their fiddles and banjos.

It was a reckless and feckless and mostly happy time, by the accounts of Hart and the men before him. A sign over a jail said, "God Bless Our Home." The lettering over a cookery spelled out YREKABAKERY, which reads the same backward and forward. Main Street, which separated the claims and quarters of Union men and Rebs, was popularly called The Mason-Dixon Line. Other occasions of mirth were peculiarly contemporary. Like most Chinese, Florence's residents, the butt of much humor, shipped their dead back to the Celestial Kingdom for burial; unlike some, they boiled the bones before freighting them off, partly because they believed that decomposing the flesh drove out the devil and partly because it was a devil of a drive out to tidewater.

There was heartbreak, too, as implied by a letter from early prospector James Fergus quoted by an early guidebook. "I do not think they (the Salmon River mines) are inviting fields at present for the general emigrant," he admonished. "There are a great many hardships to encounter in all new countries, and they become greater the further away from the borders of civilization. . . . the mountains are still in possession of numerous bands of roving Indians . . . who look upon any settler in their territory as an intruder, his goods lawful plunder, and his scalp a lawful prize. Even the seeker after gold is not always rewarded, but often after enduring hardships that he would be unwilling to endure in an old settled country, goes home poor in purse and broken in health, or toils on in search of

Despite his formidable credentials as survival expert, artisan, and wilderness historian-philosopher, Sylvan Hart is irrepressibly fond of self caricature for his infrequent visitors.

Hart's four-acre domain on Idaho's River of No Return. Flowing from lower left past his garden plot is Five Mile Creek. Blacksmith shop is at left, with living quarters to right. In upper right of picture is the bomb shelter Hart blasted out of the rock.

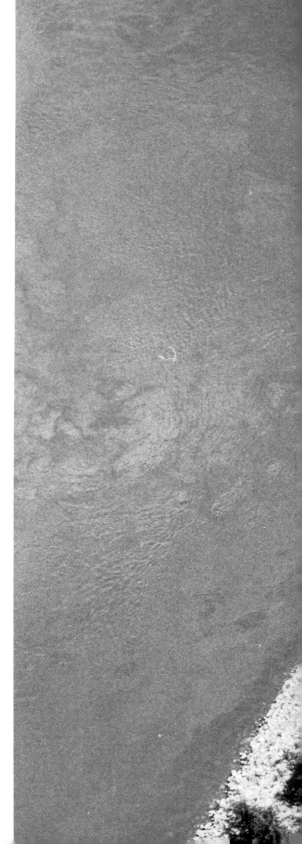

PHOTOGRAPHS BY TED STRESHINSKY FOR
Sports Illustrated.

Wearing his characteristic—and protective—summertime bearhide helmet, Hart hoes the garden in which he raises some twenty varieties of vegetables. Beyond the deer fence lie hundreds of square miles of wilderness.

Pouch and powder horns are the accoutrements of Hart's life and art.

Sylvan's pole bridge, pinned precariously to the sheer face of a cliff high above the roiling River of No Return, constitutes the only path to the outside world.

Buildings at left are Hart's adobe-walled kitchen house, storehouse, and seasonal sleeping quarters. At right, the blacksmith shop and, flying proudly, Sylvan's tattered forty-eight star flag.

Some of Hart's hand-wrought domestic ware—copper samovar, creamer, sugar bowl, ladles, pot, lamp, tea kettles, and tea ball—laid out on a table made from the flooring of a ghost-town cabin.

Detail work atop Hart's samovar. He made the eyes of the squirrels with beads which came from India.

In what he calls his "blacksmith and millinery shop," Sylvan demonstrates his smithy skill. Tools beyond counting crowd the walls and workbench.

Each of these samples of his innumerable hammers, scrapers, punches, awls, auzes, gouges, and other implements was hand-made by Hart.

Sylvan's knives, displayed here on an elkskin, are more for use than for show. Each kind has its special function.

Hart demonstrating how he accurately bores rifle barrels with a crude home-made machine. Rifling grooves are also cut with muscle power alone. The cutter, says he, comes out "smoking."

This is the pistol, with its hand-engraved stock of mountain sheep horn, that Sylvan customarily tucks into his belt on forays outside his compound.

Hart's laboriously handcrafted arsenal includes an ornately carved flintlock .45, an enormous .64, a Remington-style .50, and a sawed-off .54 with a British musket stock.

the phantom fortune, which it may never be his lot to find. . . ."

Under a stern heading, *The Reality*, Captain James Fisk, author of *Idaho: her gold fields, and the routes to them*, a fascinating and authoritative 1863 guide to the new Golconda, said, "Have a good reason for loosing from the old anchorage before going in search of a better. Do not start on such a journey with the idea that it is going to be simply a fine play-spell, and that when you get through you will tumble into some gulch and come out forthwith laden with your fortune in gold. Be content with doing well, and do not run after every big story that flits through camp. . . . None who have *homes* and a reasonable means of livelihood should be incited by stories, however true they may be, to emigrate to far off territories. Nor should any man, who, from having been born tired, or otherwise so indisposed to labor as to have always failed to obtain an honest living, ever think of succeeding in a new territory, be it rich with minerals or otherwise. The digging of gold or other precious metals is a lottery in which there are many prizes— but very many blanks. . . ."

Within ten years, every ticket was a blank. By 1874, the lowly Chinese had taken over so completely that, on Florence's main street, a Chinese flag waved in place of the Stars and Stripes, "proof in itself of decay and degeneracy, the last stage of decadence."

The fun and folly and fantasies of fortune are now all gone away. In the thirties, rather less romantic times, refugees from a sordid decade ripped up the last remnants of Florence and sifted the townsite for revalued gold, reclaiming much dust scattered in the streets and dropped through cracks in floors in the halcyon days.

Again, standing where manifest destiny passed with little trace, one is reminded of Fisk's description of Idaho before the great gold-fevered hegira: "We were wont to regard it as a waste place, to be forever surrendered to the red man and the other native tenants of the wilderness—a sacred haunt where nature should be left to revel in a solitude to be seldom, if ever, disturbed by the footstep of our intrusive race."

In the forties, often the only footsteps were those of Sylvan Hart.

6

No longer is "Florence City the largest settlement in the Salmon River country, and the general depot for supplies," as the early guidebook had it, but it remains true, in reduced degree, that "on the Clearwater river and its branches, north of the Salmon, gold is found over a large extent of country, Elk City and Oro-Fino being the principal centers of business and population."

As one approaches closer to Hart's domain, this becomes more and more unspoiled country. In season, waterfalls tumble into the canyon and enormous rocks overhang the road as it penetrates farther up the Clearwater. A road leads north to Stites and Kooskia, reminding the traveler it was between those two towns that a twentieth-century railroad extension necessitated relocating an Indian graveyard. Work halted when the crew turned up a strange-looking ball of buffalo hide. Unwinding the long strip of hide, the men found a medal presented to a chief by the Lewis and Clark Expedition.

New Golden, a forlorn handful of asphalt-papered cabins standing near the junction of Tenmile Creek three miles west and north of old Golden, was until recently distinguished by the presence of Dave Brazil, an acquaintance of Sylvan's who remembered many of the old-timers and who had a huge collection of fading pictures of prospecting, trapping, and now-vanished landmarks. Brazil died in 1967. His passing was a further reminder that the legend dies with its witnesses, leaving as only testimony a relatively few sheets of paper, flat, dimensionless, voiceless paper rapidly growing brittle, and, where we are lucky, a cyclopedic Sylvan Hart.

Just beyond New Golden, another road leads up to the old Elk City Stage Road, built and used before bulldozers made possible a way through the tortuous canyon. Sampling the old route's angry ruts and deep puddles, I remembered being told of the years when a trip to Elk City in winter was made with a sleigh and four horses, taking two days and requiring overnighting at the old staging stop called Newsome House. Snowshoes were fitted to the horses' feet, and should an animal step off the eighteen-inch-wide beaten track, it bogged down belly-deep in the snow. Long ago? Yes, if 1929 is long ago.

Elk City's central stores and outlying cabins still stand, but perhaps the best thing about Elk is its palpable air of isolation. On the busiest random weekend of summer, when tens of millions of Americans flee one place for another, the sense here is that all the clang and clamor are happening out *there* somewhere. This is definitely beyond the fresh milk and grapefruit juice of the supermarket belt. The cuisine of the one restaurant is pretty much limited to hamburger and potato chips. The only smog comes from one small sawmill on the edge of town.

Once Elk City's population was 5,000, and as many as eighty teams a night would put up at local stables and corrals on their way to the big boom at Buffalo Hump. That was only the turn of the century, recent as gold excitements go, but it seems nearly as long distant as Elk's own stampede, begun when a party from Orofino panned the first two bits' worth of gold in 1861 at the mouth of Glass Gulch. Here is how a contemporary newspaper close enough to feel the fever but secure enough not to denounce the new enthusiasm as a hoax and a brazen plot to depopulate its own metropolis reported the discovery: "When the news of the new diggings had been promulgated the store of Miner & Arnold [in Pierce] was literally besieged. As the news radiated (and it was not long in spreading), picks and shovels were thrown down, claims were deserted and turn your eye where you would you would see droves of people coming in hot haste to town; some were packing one thing on their backs and some another, all intent on scaling the mountains through frost and snow and taking up a claim in the new El Dorado. On the streets there was a perfect jam, a mass of human infatuation jostling, shoving and elbowing each other whilst the questions 'Did you know that McGill is back? Have you heard the news from up the river? Have you got a cayuse? How much are you going to take? etc.' were put to one another. Cayuse horses went up from $25 to $75 and even $100. Flour, bacon, beans, tea, coffee, sugar, frying pans, coffee pots and mining tools were instantly in demand."

That great mob enraptured with the vision of picking up mintable money like manna from the desert are now as vanished as the nuggets they sought. Their wood flumes and sluices have rotted back into the forest mold, and the hills once denuded for rough planks and mine props have regrown great stands of spruce and ponderosa. Red men no longer file through the seldom-seen groves; but neither do white men. There is no significant settlement north of Elk for 110 miles, east for at least sixty, south for at least 115.

Travel south on the thirty-one-mile road to the ghost town of Dixie, where, Sylvan remembers, as recently as 1937 500 persons collected their mail, and you travel a route where the wind wanders down the fragrant valleys mixed only with a little woodsmoke. Not even the first crude wagon road was completed up the Red and Crooked Rivers until 1897, and the euphonious towns of the Buffalo Hump to the west—Hump Town, Frog Town, Concord, Calendar —did not get their first set of wheel ruts until the twentieth century.

In winter, all freight for the burgeoning communities bunched near the head of Whistling Pig Canyon was towed up on big toboggans. If today's visitor cannot conjure a picture of icy isolation, of ultramarine nightfall blueing the snow-carpeted gulches while afterglow still tinted North Pole Mountain a frosty sherbet orange, one man's recollection will. "The night camp at Fish Lake [at the mouth of Whistling Pig], used as a swing camp for sledders and packers from each end of the trail, was as comfortable as canvas, blankets, sourdough bread and beans could make it, and we had a good cook." So wrote Gardiner Porter, a near-anonymous native of the country, remembering the pleasure of huddled human warmth in wilderness in a little tract preserved at the Grangeville library. "Tents, buried in the snow, Sibley stoves, brush beds on the ground, seven or more in a bed, where, if one wanted to turn over, everyone turned at the signal 'flop!' On colder (they were all cold) nights, watches kept the Sibley going. Several of these men later made fortunes from the Buffalo Hump mines, but not one died with money. . . ."

Nevada Jack, one of those veterans who had been packing and wrangling since they wore three-cornered chaps, figured in a present-century story of the Hump's colder season that I had read. (The region was said to have only two—winter and the Fourth of July.) Sledding the mail from Adams Camp to Calendar, Jack often struggled in yards-deep snow. "One evening, after a heartbreaking day in soft snow," the story goes, "he pulled into a mining camp still several miles from the end of his 'star route.' A Boston lady, wife of a resident engineer, appeared on a porch normally about fourteen feet above the ground but now on a level with the sled, gazed tearfully upon and spoke sympathetically to 'the poor dear little doggies,' went back into her house and reappeared with a plate of doughnuts. [It should here be noted that doughnuts, called bear tracks or bear sign, were the great delicacy of the earlier West.] Jack numbly watched the exotic dainties disappear into the dogs. Finally he could take it no longer. 'Lady,' he exploded, 'I've come as far as these poor little doggies, they haven't had to break trail or herd me, and the coffee that should have gone with those sinkers wouldn't have poisoned me.' "

A way south and west, Hundred Dollar Jim, so called because on each of his infrequent trips to town he would bet exactly one hundred dollars in gold dust on the same number of the roulette wheel, was killed by a similar sled in similar terrain. Missing for some time, he was sought by a search party and finally sighted harnessed into the traces of his own sled, pulling it across a mountainside. As the party, minutes late, watched in horror, Jim's struggles loosed the mass of snow, avalanching him hundreds of feet down into a lake below—a lake named Dollar Lake.

Buffalo Hump was the home of Bill Borden, a man of such ambitious thirst that after drinking Hump bars dry, he regularly scheduled expeditions down to Boise, according to another story often heard in this area. There, to abet the grandeur of his binges, he bought the best bedroom set in the city and had it installed in the Boise jail. Each time he came to Boise for a bender thereafter, he telegraphed ahead to have that particular cell reserved.

It is also said to have been the locale for the nameless drunk who staggered out of a saloon one evening and wandered into the town graveyard, where he lay him down to sleep. Waking next morning, he sat up, blinking, and looked around in utter astonishment. "Resurrection, by God!" he exclaimed, "and *me* the first bloody bugger awake!"

And lastly, there is the tale of Jim Helmsworth, a story to make the blood run both hot and cold. At work in a mine in this country, Helmsworth was tending the shaft head while two comrades loaded ore at the bottom. As he hoisted one bucket, the crank of the windlass broke. The heavily laden iron bucket began plummeting toward the men below. Helmsworth thrust his arm hard between the spinning teeth of the meshing cogwheels, which slowly ground to a halt after mashing the flesh and bone of his arm all the way to the shoulder. The miners below were saved.

Now, in 1969, once again only narrowing trails lead to

Calendar, Hump Town, Frog Town, and Concord. Even the ghosts sleep.

Thirteen miles south of Elk City on the Dixie Road, due east of the ghost town of Orogrande, lies the last important road intersection on the way to Hart's place, a junction with one of America's more romantic thoroughfares. There a huge Forest Service sign reads in large, portentous letters:

Montana Road
STOP

WARNING
Red River-West Fork of the Bitterroot Road
Elk City, Idaho–Darby, Montana
Slow, Steep, Narrow Mountain Road
Through Uninhabited Area

Next gas station—Darby, Montana, 105 miles
Second and low gear road, 8 hours driving time
Be sure your fuel tank is full. Extra gas adviseable
Axe, shovel, bucket; essential at all times
Slides or windfalls may be encountered
BE CAREFUL

WARNING
HUNTERS

Early snows may close
this road at any time
PROCEED AT
YOUR OWN RISK

On oil company maps, this boulevard does appear, labeled "Very Poor Road." That is a matter of opinion. But the sign does mean every word, and it doesn't hurt to read a lot between the lines, too.

This is very roughly the route of the old Nez Percé Trail east across the wild, wild Selway River, the Salmon River

Breaks Primitive Area and the scarcely tame Bitterroot Range to the Big Hole and Beaverhead Valleys in Montana. Looking east down that splendid road reminds one of the early account of the Nez Percé Indian (pierced nose, in cognate French) who made E. D. Pierce the pioneer of the whole Idaho gold rush back in 1860 by innocently telling him a strange story. "One night three of us camped in a canyon far up a river," the Indian narrated. "The moon came up over the Bitter Roots and as its beams struck the western wall of the canyon we saw something like a star gleaming in the rocky cliff. We were frightened. It looked to us like the eye of the Great Spirit. We ran away. Next morning we went back there. It was a great shining ball like the white man's beads. We tried to dig it out, but it was heavy and hard. It is still there but we have forgotten the place." It is still there now. No one found the place. Perhaps some night, when Sylvan is camped at just the right spot and the moon reaches a certain point in the sky. . . .

Nez Percé used the trail to travel from winter quarters to summer, from camp to hunting ground; soon after the above ingenuous tale, whites used it as a route to Elk and Bannack and Alder Gulch. After following the ridge line between the Clearwater and the Salmon, the trail dipped deep to ford the Selway, where it branched. The northern branch crossed the Divide once near the present road and again at Lost Trail and Gibbons Passes. Just beyond the latter, retreating Chief Joseph fought the Battle of the Big Hole.

To reconstruct the arduous journey of the argonauts from east to west, or indeed to retrace the voyaging of Hart's own ancestors to Kansas and Oklahoma, it is necessary only to consult again Captain Fisk and his 1863 guide to the Idaho gold fields. "I have a few plain blunt words to submit," the good man counseled, "to those who contemplate emigrating:

"On the central route from Omaha, you should start by the fifteenth or twentieth of May.

"By steamer up the Missouri, you should leave St. Louis by the first of May.

"On the northern route, all parties should be at St. Cloud, Minnesota, the place of rendezvous, by the first of June.

". . . all should be well armed. You should move in parties of one hundred or more. Keep vigilant watch of stock and camp at night. On the march keep your train together and move in regular order.

"Whenever possible you should camp so as to form a corral of all your wagons.

"No man who makes a long overland journey is independent of those with whom he is traveling; but there should be from first to last a realizing sense of your mutual dependence. Leave no neighbor behind in distress. Choose a leader and respect always the rules he may deem necessary to establish.

". . . no person should migrate overland to the mountains with less than (9) nine months' supplies. Take plenty of such staple items as flour, bacon or charside meat, beans, mixed vegetables, groceries, etc.; and do not lug along chairs, bureaus or bedsteads.

"Your spare funds invested before you start in the necessaries of life, tobacco, ammunition, boots and shoes, etc., will bring at the end of your journey at least five hundred per cent advance.

"The cheapest and best teams for your freight-wagons are well-broke, young, short-bodied, solid cattle, with muscle and motion, and when possible there should be three yoke to the wagon. These teams will outlast horses or mules, and in any event will thrive so as to make good beef.

"The thimble-skame, Yankee or Michigan style of wagon, well-covered, is the best for general use for freight, and no wagon should be loaded heavier than two thousand pounds."

Scraps and pieces of Captain Fisk's account of his own '62 expedition over a similar route lends equal insight into a pioneer state of mind: "On leaving St. Paul on the 16th (sixteenth) of June, I had unfurled, from a staff lashed to the front of the express-wagon, which led the train, the national colors; and I am proud to say, that it every day floated to the breeze, from the Mississippi to the Columbia, and no man insulted it.

"We had here the pleasure of joining the officers and soldiers of the fort [Abercrombie] and the settlers of that neighborhood, in an appropriate celebration of the anniversary of our national independence, before starting on our long journey, the greatest deprivation of which was the suspense under which we must remain for months as to the progress of our arms in crushing the rebellion that would undo the great act of ('76) seventy-six."

"Captain Fisk having resolved not to travel on Sundays. . . .

"At this camp [second crossing of the Shayenne] occurred an incident which served to break the monotony of camp-life, and to consecrate the spot in our memories. . . . A young couple had been observed, early in our journey, to evince a strong and growing affection for each other . . . and determined to celebrate their nuptials with all the forms and solemnities that the absence of municipal organization would permit." The two were married "with the moon shedding a bright, chaste light over the scene," followed by "a dance upon the green sward to the music of violins."

"A child was born in our camp last night, and has been added to our list of emigrants. Should this young pioneer become a character in the world's history, it occurs to me that it will puzzle its admirers and followers to point out his birthplace."

Company met on the long and lonely trail was usually of a sort unlikely to be cultivated for membership in gentlemen's clubs of the East. Of the mountain Blackfeet, Fisk recorded, "Mr. Meldrum, who has spent thirty (30) years among the Indians, says he once found in a medicine lodge a basket containing sixty (60) first-joints of fingers, which they had cut from their own hands during the 'making medicine.' "

In this country, in this mood, in gathering darkness, proceed south toward Sylvan Hart and his River of No Return. Climb the winding, deep-ditched road over Jack Mountain divide and down to the old placer workings along Crooked Creek after dark. God be thanked, there are no lights anywhere. The loudest sound: occasionally, rushing water. Entering it before you realize, you reach the little townsite of Dixie where Fourth of July Creek tumbles down off the mountain. Tall, rusted antique gas pumps loom up in the middle of the road. A couple of false fronts stand sentinel. One light burns. Saloon, cafe, hostelry in one little room, Dixie's one house of business looks, like all such lit places in dark, forgotten towns, at once frightened and frightening in its aloneness. Casting one square of light into blackness, such a place is either a single uncertain candle in the wilderness or capital of a world. And both.

Let us conjecture. Suppose, if you can, that Chinese bombs have some time since melted the cities outside. Now you are a wanderer stumbling into such a place—a Bodie, California; a Garnet, Montana; a St. Elmo, Colorado. There are still scores of such. In the authentic meaning of Locke and Mill, the two or three inhabitants of such a place would live under the rule of natural law. Theirs and theirs alone would be the decision to help or to harm, to be helped or to be hurt. One outsider entering in would alter the entire equation of morality. Indeed, were the present United States not so excessively ordered, litigious, and regimented, even now dwellers in such places would largely be governed by individual conscience; and the whole experience of the United States, at very least, has been that the greater the latitude for exercise of conscience, the greater its strength. In any event, those who did not like the prevailing morality and customs could leave, or change them.

Another feeling evoked by so simple, rare, and delightful

76

a thing as an underpopulated town is a gratifying sense of independence, a heady unboundness that makes one wish to spurn even the small and innocent creature comforts this kind of place might have to offer, to continue on down the dark road, to be a stranger passing through in the night, bound for the uninhabitedness beyond. Better to ramble on into the blackness, peering up creeks and gulches with aromatic names or no names at all in search of a good place for an impromptu camp, a jack camp. Here is an adequate spot, down near where Thousand Dollar Gulch runs into Crooked Creek.

Strange to lie in a sleeping bag and look almost straight up the one-hundred-foot bole of a ponderosa pine to the black, star-strewn sky, the sky a dark silk canopy punched full of holes that let light through in specks and dots and pinpricks. Strange to see the black boughs of the pine radiate outward in a ragged-edged circle, forming and reforming new free-form shapes in the soughing breezes. Strange to be so alone in a world containing such urban abnormalities as New York and Calcutta.

It is a vanishing luxury to wake undisturbed in the morning and see blossoms of wildflowers swaying above one's eyes, to roll up a sleeping bag and dress in the warm early sun, getting one's feet a little wet in the cool water of the dew and to ride on through enclosing forest unmet for hours. After such seclusion, it is almost startling to burst into bright sunlight and a view so sweeping it is as if you see the whole world at once.

This, California Point, is the first real view of the Salmon canyon. Five miles on is Cove Saddle, where one can look down and see both east and west for miles. Shortly beyond begin seven miles of switchbacks, twisting continuously down and down and down into the canyon. Clamp on the brakes and squeal slowly down, stopping sometimes to cool the fading brakes. Try not to roll off the narrow ledge, for the result would be to bounce, roll, and fall 3,600 feet.

Arriving safely at the bottom, I wriggled my pack on and

set out across the narrow bridge spanning the Salmon River just above Mackay Bar. The trail to Sylvan's place started steeply up a rocky slope, and I quickly learned that the unmaintained track was not the good path it had looked from the river. It soon commenced to wind along the lip of a sharp drop-off. Between negotiating around the large rocks, looking for snakes, and taking care not to let a fairly heavy pack overbalance me over the edge, progress was slower and more tiring than the relatively easy walking I had expected. The shadeless hillside began to create an impression that the afternoon was not only hot, as I had recognized despite my eagerness to get to Five Mile, but *quite* hot. The first effective shade, a friendly ponderosa, was too welcome to ignore.

At the edge of the pretty little glade marking Three Mile Creek's course down the mountain, I stopped again, unshrugging my pack and sitting down to rest. When the path curved around to approach the creek, I looked for a good place to drink. A series of little pools beckoned, wholly overhung by willows and vines and all other kinds of vegetation native here. Beneath, Three Mile Creek ran cold, green, and mossy. Flopping luxuriously down on my stomach, I drank, icing my nose in the cool current. As I drank, I studied the variegated patterns of the moss on the marbled granite, almost magnified by the crystal liquid, and both smelled and tasted the green organic flavor the moss gave to the clear water. After slaking the dryness, I rolled over on my back and listened to the murmuring, sucking, slurred talk of the creek—then drank again.

Having passed the unoccupied cabin which gives the place its name, Ludwig's, I crossed the creek on stepping stones. Just at my chosen crossing place, a black and a red raspberry shrub grew prodigiously lushly and equally thornily in a tiny islet. At the cost of a couple of scratches, I picked some berries, sipped more cold, clear water and felt well repaid for my walk.

Then, coming on some plump currants, I passed through

a very small and long-abandoned orchard. Most of the trees were dead or deteriorated, but one or two looked as if they would confer tangy apples on the next passer-by. From here, the trail sloped downward. I began to hope that it would henceforth follow a nice water grade. Not so. Soon, it dipped sharply down to a little beach, which it crossed, and then ended abruptly in a lot of rocks. Assuming there had been a slide, I and my pack teetered from rock to rock for some distance. Finally, long after it should have been obvious to anyone less stubborn, I admitted that the path would not resume. The choice was going back (unthinkable!), clambering up the mountainside (impossible at this point) or going ahead until the trail (if there still was one) dropped down toward the river again.

Going forward, the rocks became larger and larger, and more and more jumbled, often tilting and slipping. Driftwood and fallen tree boles became mixed in, like big jackstraws in some untidy giant-child's pile of blocks and marbles. Ridiculously weakened by six years of living in New York, I now tired very rapidly. Mad and frustrated, I tried clawing up the slope. Over tangled fallen timber, it was futile. I stopped and sprawled out, exhausted.

When I continued, it was only far enough to see that no familiar stretch of trail lay around the next bend, or the next. At this rate of traveling, it would be dark and I would be played out before I got to Sylvan's. After sad consideration of the shorter, harder way forward and the longer way back, I chose to turn back. Arriving at Mackay as tired, hungry and hot as I've ever been, I discovered that the temperature in the shade, in early evening, was 106 degrees.

And, somehow, I was pleased that the trail from Five Mile Bar to the nearest summer habitation was not the easy trip I had thought it, that Hart is something more than just arm's length from even the most rustic evidences of the twentieth century.

$\lll\lll$ 7

NEXT MORNING, I again arrived at Five Mile Bar by boat. Somewhat surprisingly, Sylvan was not in the slightest censorious or supercilious about the failed hike in. "Lost the trail down below, did you?" he said. "It *is* deceiving. The real trail goes way high on the mountainside at Ludwig's and is much fainter than the one down to the river. Those rocks and that driftwood are the very worst kind of walking anywhere."

"You didn't bring my champagne, did you?" he asked, losing interest in my wrong turn. "I'm kind of expecting a bottle. I was planning to present a soldier named Fenstermacher with it and a garland when he came from Vietnam. That's about all a war hero can expect anymore."

Even for a visitor boasting neither champagne nor campaign, Hart did not neglect his usual huge hospitality, which in its initial, positively manic stages consisted as always of large doses of history, autobiography, and a high-powered guided tour. As always, there were quantities of new things to see and hear, partly because Buckskin had done some more manufacturing and partly because even a frequent visitor will always have missed a lot on previous trips. And frequency in this country means once a year.

Within the first few minutes, one had seen a grindstone run by a kind of homemade bicycle mechanism, a chair made entirely of elk antlers, an entire box of medicine brought in back in '33 and never used. "Not even an aspirin," he maintained. "Once you get some sourdough you don't need any more medicine." He also displayed a splendid broad, double-edged sword. The sword handle, Bill explained, was a classic fishscale pattern. It actually came off a broken U.S. Cavalry sword he had found, but it could as well be Roman or Viking, for the pattern was thousands of years old. It was like hats. All the good hat patterns had been devised in the Middle Ages or before, Sylvan says, so all we can use are medieval throwaways.

A sizeable portion of Buckskin's winter had been spent carving a complete set of utensils and dishware from cherrywood. Proudly pointing out that six different colors could be seen in the smooth wood, he exhibited samples: a beer mug, plates, forks, spoon ladle, cup, bowl, dish, clamps, mortar and pestle, wine cup, lemon squeezer, and a whimsical pie crust crimper that spells out, "More pie, Louise," along the rim of the crust. The first pie decorated therewith, he said, had incorporated thirteen yellowheaded blackbirds. That was probably a joke, but a certain reluctance to ask took hold. Too many such jokes turn out to be—also— true.

"A lot of good culture was lost in the Civil War," Bill said. "Before that, everything that could be made out of wood, was. Then along came all those cannon factories, and a lot of them converted to making ironware after the war."

He had chosen cherry because of the slight taste. To demonstrate, he squeezed a couple of lemons he happened to have. The last little bit of lemonade did indeed taste faintly of cherry. Maybe it was that flavor that made it seem so exotically good, or maybe it was the extreme unexpectedness of sipping lemonade, cooled with cold brook water, in the deep backwoods of Idaho. Certainly the whole fruit, lying bright yellow on the weathered table, looked as foreign as breadfruit or mangoes.

Savoring this rare import, Sylvan told how he had spent

the winter fighting off uninvited bears. Since the preceding summer and fall had been poor seasons for food, the bears had tended to wake up mad and hungry in the middle of their hibernations. The Hart garden became a popular nighttime target. Bill would rise, scantily clad, and shoot at them offhand from fifty hards or so. He couldn't kill 'em at that range, he said, but he could show 'em what his feelings were. The climax came when a particularly brazen bear, in broad daylight, knocked down the gate, marched into the pantry and began sorting through the groceries. That invasion of privacy really angered Bill. Yelling and hollering, he ran the bear out, adding a bullet through the heart for emphasis.

Incidentally, there was a witness, and he told exactly the same story. It would have sounded farther-fetched had Buckskin not had similar bear problems before. A previous black bear raided the garden, broke down an apricot tree, and finally started tearing down the chicken pen, terrifying Bill's little banties. You don't *have* to believe all Buckskin's stories, but you ought to.

Mountain sheep bring their little lambs down to Five Mile Bar. Does give birth to their fawns right here. Sylvan will indicate the place. In winter, avocets and blackbirds land at the bar so tired they just stand there for a day, motionless. Several times lightning has struck so close to him he could smell ozone extremely strongly, but "all I've been knocked into is a crouch." Eagles, on rare occasion, will grab each other's claws and cartwheel through the air, emitting the most curdling screams, but they are merely playing. Hart attests to it.

Disbelief, or perhaps simply incomprehension, is a common reaction to Bill and what he says. Shaken by his easy familiarity with what they think impossible, some few people, men in particular, possibly because they are somehow made to feel inadequate, call Buckskin a faker and a fraud. Men who couldn't drive a woodscrew through soft pine call him, with relief, a charlatan because they have found one mass-produced item in his compound. People who would have a hard time surviving if beyond reach of the simplest mechanical devices sometimes scorn his passion for self-sufficiency as a retreat from reality.

Just how out of phase with some of his contemporaries Sylvan is was amply demonstrated by the first rubber rafters down the Salmon the year before last, a Sierra Club group. The Sierra Club is one of our final and best conservationist hopes, but this particular bunch included a disproportionate number of city yokels. One carefully looked over Buckskin's big garden, inspected his smoked and salted bear and elk meat, surveyed his cubic yards of elaborate craftsmanship, and asked, "What do you do for a living?" That left even Bill speechless.

He was better prepared for the next one. "What do you do all day?" a sweet middle-aged thing asked. "Well, I have lots of little projects," Buckskin roared quietly. "There's Schubert. He never finished that symphony, you know, and I was thinking of helping him out."

Funny thing was, as soon as he said it, you could see Sylvan beginning to think it wasn't a bad idea. At some later time, he might be deeply absorbed in the study of musical theory.

Yet, as always, Hart was not only unfailingly polite but genuinely happy to troop the visitors around and explain again things he has explained a hundred times. Watching, you began to suspect that his long years in the wilderness have afforded so much opportunity for storing up patience and so little opportunity for disillusioning himself with daily human friction that, remaining where and as he is, his rare visitors were incapable of altogether exhausting his patience.

Some time after the float trippers had drifted downstream, Sylvan put in the Dutch oven a batch of biscuits made with vinegar, vanilla, rum, and no soda. While they baked, he reminisced about his earlier life and how it led to Five Mile Bar.

At my request, he brought out a couple of old pictures, their blacks turning brown and their whites yellow. The first was a photograph of his father. "I was a much more fancy-looking kid than that," Sylvan chuckled, with mingled pride and self-disbelief. He then showed a picture of himself as an angelic-looking six-year-old with long, very fine blond hair. I registered the expected surprise. Sylvan opened an envelope and pulled out a lock of that same fine baby hair.

I said that I was surprised by the blond hair because all the pictures and engravings of Harts I had seen in genealogical libraries had shown them exactly like a contemporary description of Revolution-era Harts: "rather above a medium size, dark-complexioned with dark hair and eyes." Many of those eighteenth- and nineteenth-century ancestors, in fact, had shown an eerily precise resemblance to twentieth-century Sylvan. So exactly duplicated were the eagle eyes, prominent foreheads, large ears, long noses, ruddy cheeks, balding pates, and strong mouths that one could have been looking at a photograph of their descendant. Even the growth of the beard and the pattern of recession of the hairline were the same. It was rather like meeting a modern Virginian named Tom Jefferson and discovering that he had the third president's identical wild red hair, blue eyes, high cheekbones, and a long, thin nose, just like the nose on the nickel.

Sylvan Ambrose agreed that all related Harts seemed surprisingly alike, physically and otherwise. "An old, old family tradition says that Harts shoot well, run well, and have sharp pocketknives," he said. "All your good marksmen generally have a dark eye and a pretty good-size one. Of course, only part of it is heredity. The rest is training. Now, if a tree falls off that mountain over there I notice it right away, but at first it was all just a mass of rocks and trees. It takes a good eye *and* training to know there's a bear over there because a black speck is out of place.

"There are two other families of Harts in Idaho, incidentally, but they're Cornishmen, and badly hated for clannishness. All Cousin Jacks are clannish, but it's a good stock. If you're Cornish, there's a good chance of your being part Phoenician, which were an enterprising lot and had been civilized a long time."

When I was able to steer him back to the old Indian Territory, Sylvan happily spoke of his childhood. He talked about how when he was a kid in still sparsely populated Oklahoma he seldom had other children to play with, about how he would get lost on little expeditions. He had a favorite little creek, running through a brush-covered ravine, and he used to go up that for miles, sometimes encountering animals, buffalo bones, arrowheads, and "a little prehistoric stuff." He still remembers his biggest childhood disillusionment. Meeting a real, genuine buffalo hunter who chanced to visit his home, young Sylvan Ambrose was thrilled—until he discovered his hero had frozen feet. [Not taking care of your feet is the mark of the aptly named tenderfoot.] Sylvan started hunting at the age of ten and during high school he worked at field butchering. Thus he learned something about handling meat, a knowledge he thinks is one of the two essentials lacking to most people who might like to follow his way of life. The other is blacksmithing, without which he would need a lathe to do the gunwork he does. When he was studying engineering, engineers were still required to take a course in that disappearing craft.

If there had been no such place as the Salmon River to come to, Hart believes he would have become a craftsman or a skilled mechanic in as rural a place as possible, because of his love of making things with his hands. Anything more regimenting, he says, would have resulted in his "gradually turning to stone."

"You go to work in one of those places, for someone else," he explains, "and you're caught in a situation where no matter how uninteresting something is, you have to do it. That kills your ability to take interest in anything.

"As for a desk job, it's like prison life. Physical activity—or lack of it—eats on your mental activity. Besides, here I am, sixty-one and young and eager, yet already I would've gotten my watch and been run off."

As it was, young Sylvan was seized with a bit of wanderlust. One summer after high school, like thousands of other hoboes of the restless twenties, seventeen-year-old Sylvan hopped a freight train bound for his own Big Rock Candy Mountain, with intermediate stops in Texas and Nebraska. It would be a dreary life now, but then all the states were different, and each town and locality had its own life, its own personality. Men born in surprisingly advantageous circumstances could be tempted to leave home and family by a chiming, lonesome train whistle in the night. It was the time of the bindlestiff. "I actually *saw* people carrying their clothes in a round calico bundle at the end of a forked stick," Sylvan remembers.

Young Hart traveled from wheat harvest to wheat harvest by boxcar, living in town parks, which were opened to camping during harvest time. Farmers, who competed to attract the bindlestiffs, would come by and pick up workers. For ten cents, Sylvan recalls, amused, you could buy a soup-bone with a lot of meat on it.

But coal smoke and steam and click of wheels clattering past endless lonely sidings did not get into his blood permanently. He returned to study at the University of Oklahoma, majoring in English and graduating in '31, a hard year. After working as a roughneck in an East Texas oilfield for a year, he went with his father to Idaho to placer mine, starting at historic Idaho City.

Just about the biggest, best, and brawlingest of all the commonwealth's boom towns starting up in the 1860s, Idaho City, sixty-five years before the Harts' arrival, had had four theaters, four hotels, ten Chinese laundries, and forty-one saloons. Forty million dollars in gold were taken out in sixties, but the town by no means entirely withered after that. Since the seventies, the Basin district has produced another sixty million. Such wealth bred violence. The old Territorial jail, first clink in Idaho, saw many a hanging. Two are especially fondly remembered to this day. In 1868, Simeon Walters killed Joe Bacon and threw the weighted corpse in a deep part of the Snake River. He would have escaped the gallows, too, had not Bacon's glass eye washed up on an island. In 1898, Herman St. Clair had his neck stretched for the murder of one John Decker, an execution for which engraved invitations were sent out. They read:

> Mr. _____ _____
> You are requested to be present
> at the execution of
> H. C. St. Clair
> on June 24th, 1898, at 10 A.
> M; at Idaho City, Idaho.
> J. A. Lippincott
> Not transferable   Sheriff

In fact, of the two-hundred-odd deceased buried in the Idaho City boot hill in 1863, only twenty-eight died of natural causes.

What impressed Sylvan was the disappearance of the Chinamen. Chinese, as elsewhere, had replaced white men after collapse of the early booms. One day, the Celestials of Idaho City all packed off and vanished forever. "Nobody broke into those cabins for twenty years to find out why. And then it was still a mystery. Nobody knows yet."

Finding only a little gold under a flume, the Harts moved to the Salmon River, near Five Mile. "Some guys over at Rabbit Creek, near Idaho City, were positively heroic. They were able to make a living," Sylvan recalls. "They were the only ones."

Salmon River was not vastly better, but the Harts got by. Five dollars a day was about the average, "but at least it was real honest money—Hoover dollars. Besides, if you were a bachelor and got a job, you'd feel there was some married man and his family who needed it more. Mining gold, you were *making* money, not taking it away from somebody.

"We always used sluice boxes. Never had anything rich enough to need a rocker. We were inexperienced, but there were people there to tell you how, and once you've seen gold you'll never mistake it."

Sylvan paused. "I'll say this," he said. "Placer mining produced better Americans than any other we ever had. To get a start, you only had to ask another man how much he was making. He was honest and would tell you exactly. You would ask him if there was any good place nearby. He'd say, 'Why, shore, right over there. I'll show you.' He was independent, he moved enough not to get set in his ways, and he was honest enough to have few prejudices about anything."

Sylvan's younger brother Tom joined him on the Salmon for a short while, and those were good times. "I was on a little expedition with Tom once," Sylvan remembers, eyes twinkling. "We were short on provisions and just slept out under a tree. I woke up in the morning and there was a grouse right over Tom's head in the tree. I shot its head off with a twenty-two, and it landed an inch from his head. He woke up and yelled, 'What's that!' 'Just breakfast is served, that's all,' I said.

"There were some great old characters here then. Henry Smith, a famous old miner, and his brother had a mine on Warren Summit. Their miners got paid every night, and they came down to town to spend it every night, too. There were Tom and Charlie Carpenter, who found the Mammoth Mine. There were the McDonald boys, whose father ran a saloon up at Concord. The house my nephew Rodney is building for when he visits is actually a reassembling of a house built by a famous old character named Jackson who built the first stamp mill around here. A few of those people are still around. Pete Klinghammer—he's middle-aged, seventy-five or so—lives down at the Shepp Ranch. Otis

Morse, whose father was in the Sheepeater War and who used to be at Warren, is now at Eagle. Ted Mossberger and Ken Williams, who runs the Pickell store, are at Warren. Shorty Medillo is at Dixie. Jack Taylor is at Grangeville. So is Red Harlan, at the old folks' home. He spent his life on Papoose Creek looking for gold just on the rumor that some squaw wanted to tell the whites there was gold on it and the bucks didn't want them to. Now isn't that a great piece of information?

"I hiked to Florence once back then," Buckskin continued. "We panned, and you could see what the gold was like: coarse pieces of it, and the bedrock was only two feet down, so that was quite a place to prospect.

"I was up to the Wise Boy Mine, too, quite an out of the way place. Found a magazine that said things was really humming in Detroit. Fifty people had bought automobiles that year.

"It was Ernest Oberbillig's brother that named me Buckskin Bill in '38, when I showed up at Mackay Bar in a deerskin jacket. He was partly thinking of Buckskin Frank Leslie, who used to be around Tombstone and is supposed to have killed Johnny Siringo, the lone cowboy who made a career of knocking off outlaws for years. I was 'bout the same height, build, and appearance. As for the Bill, if you're out in the West and not some kind of Bill, that's bad. Better to be Willy or Billy, the diminutive, than no Bill at all.

" 'Course, the government turns it around to Bill Buckskin. That looks more like a name to them, you see. People send mail to Buckskin Charlie, Buckskin Joe, I still get it. They send it to Riggins, Dixie, Warren, Salmon City, I *still* get it."

That brought Hart's thoughts around to the present. To the extent, in fact, that as he sat mixing a sauce of evaporated milk, egg yolk, cumin, and olive oil, he veered off to cover the Israeli-Arab War. "A lot of the Egyptians were barefoot, and it seems like a barefoot army can hardly ever

90

win," he declared. "Besides, a lot of those Russian trucks overheated in the Sinai desert because they still had shields over their radiators to protect them from cold weather." Bill also had some advice to offer on the Army's M–16 rifle, which he had read about in the *Wall Street Journal*. (Sylvan gets much of his news of the outside world from the *Journal*, a periodical to which his stock-analyst nephew was sure he ought to have a gift subscription. The papers accumulate in a homemade washtub until Bill gets around to reading a couple of weeks' worth. Buckskin's nephew was also certain that Bill ought to have a two-way radio. Hart politely accepted the gift, and the next time young Rodney visited, the radio was hidden away unassembled deep under last year's elk skins and bear grease. There it has remained, totally unused.)

Old gunmaker Buck couldn't say from experience whether the M–16 jammed or not; *his* objection was that it had a sight that stuck up so far you had to expose too much of your head and shoulders to aim it.

This led to discussion of physical deficiencies in the jets used in Vietnam and of the philosophical fallacies of jets in general. Hart admitted that Air Force jets now sometimes rattle this last wilderness with sonic booms. My own objections to this kind of intrusion seemed well summarized by Thoreau: "Thank God, men cannot as yet fly, and lay waste the sky as well as the earth!" But Sylvan was more mild, and he minded the military jets hardly at all. "Better to listen to sonic booms than eat fishheads and rice with chopsticks in a few years," he said.

That shut up the visiting preacher for quite a while, or at least long enough to eat dinner. By talking less and listening and observing more, the visitor discovered more of those details which make life on Five Mile educational. Finding that the drinking water had gone warm, Sylvan simply poured it over the dirt floor. This had the additional advantage of nicely settling any dust. In one move, Hart had demonstrated his independence of both sink and broom. "I put in a new clay floor recently," he said. "It eventually wears down to the beach sand, and the wind blows that around."

This was opportunity to notice for the first time the roof grounded in case of lightning and the shutter closeable over the only large window in the winter quarters. It was time, too, to see the sewing horse, with foot-operated clamp, for making buckskin and leather goods; sheep-horn stirrups; and the firebreak, ditch, and wall around the outside of the stockade. Bill explained that protection against fire was part of the reason for the separation between his buildings and that for the same reason he would never roof with new shakes over old. The old ones would get dry and tinderlike.

The shingles reminded Sylvan of a story about two local prospectors and their fat partner. Since their friend was both grossly corpulent and a grievous tenderfoot, the thinner men left him to tend their cabin and garden while they spent the summer searching for gold. Tiring of the routine, and feeling he was not doing quite his full share, the fat man hit on the idea of surprising his partners by replacing the cabin's leaky roof. Each day, during a long stretch of good weather, he dragged himself up a ladder and painstakingly applied a few shingles. Happily, he finally finished the job the day before his partners were to return and just as a storm was obviously building up in the west. By good luck, his delighted friends appeared as the storm was breaking, and all three ducked into the fine new shelter.

The neatly made roof leaked like a sieve. When the rain let up, the prospectors rushed outside to see what was wrong. They discovered that their partner had started his rows of shingles at the top instead of the bottom. Therefore all the shingles, instead of overlapping to let the water run off, lapped under each other, each forming a little V-shaped trough perfectly suited to collect water. The fat man had put the roof on upside down.

The breezes of evening began stirring as the sun slid down behind the mountains. Sylvan pulled over a Stonebridge lantern, nothing more than a candle in a collapsible case. "See how much better this is than a flashlight," he said. "You can't *ever* supply yourself with enough flashlight batteries, no matter how many you bring. Just like tobacco." He talked again of how he had lived in a willow tepee at Mackay Bar one summer, of how he had slept in a trench covered with pine boughs when he first came to Five Mile.

As the dusk thickened toward impenetrability, we glanced out to the river and saw a multipointed buck strolling across the beach a few yards away, regarding us with the merest flicker of interest. We stopped talking to watch. The buck exhausted his mild curiosity about us, turned his head to look at the river, got bored, and started sauntering off in another direction. We watched until, no longer contrasting with the blued sand, he merged into the deep green woods. He had obviously never been shot at in all his life.

A tiny movement in the dark near us caught the corner of my eye. Buckskin's house toad had come out to clean up the bugs. Bill said he had had a beaver that came out exactly at 3:30 P.M. each day to cut willows, and that a previous toad had emerged for bug patrol at precisely five minutes to six. You could not really see the toad but more simply sensed its presence. That put us, the toad, and the insects all on approximately the same footing.

And so to bed. Nice to have that regularity, one supposes, and nicer yet to have not a single foolish thing to stay up to worry over. It seemed a shame, perhaps, not to stay effortlessly drinking the languorously liquid air, yet the very abundance of the supply encouraged moderation.

As always, Sylvan would insist, with a hardheaded generosity brooking no such foolishness as a refusal, on the visitor's taking the best place to sleep. Nothing to do but mop one's face lightly with a washcloth in cold water, climb the stairs, and sprawl out luxuriously on top of a down sleeping bag on Sylvan's balcony. An occasional sly zephyr would tickle the toes to remind you where you were, and then you would fall quickly asleep. At some hour, each night, the briskening air would send you burrowing into the sleeping bag for comfort, waking barely long enough to gratefully register the star-dripping sky in some corner of the mind.

Each morning at Five Mile, that strange alarum, the hoarse screech of a rooster—half homely and familiar and evocative of boyhood days spent on an Illinois blackland farm, half cry of a wild bird recently penned in an attempt at domestication by a nomad-peasant himself scarcely tame—wakens the day. Freer birds have been rustling and twittering and caroling for some time, of course, but the intent laze-abed can easily screen out those musical sounds. The howling of that confounded rooster, however, at the very first false dawn, can not be ignored.

This is a city reaction. When one does tentatively open one eye, it instantly becomes apparent that no soot will fall off the lashes. No trucks grind and roar on any street. There is no commuter train to catch. No newspaper will catalog yesterday's disasters. It's a perfectly beautiful 1768 morning and damn the British.

The warming morning smells pleasantly of flowers and forthcoming heat. Buckskin is already making breakfast, which features fried summer squash. Fried squash, it turns out, tastes better when you eat it with a long, two-tined Civil War era tin fork with buffalo-horn handle reclaimed from the gold rush. Hart has a very complete service of these things, and at that he selected only the best he found. Many of the others were very poor, he said, being merely

95

stamped hastily out of tin-can stock to supply the rush from its own refuse and so avoid the expense of shipping wares west.

"I'm a vegetarian if that's all I've got," Sylvan proclaimed. "You might call that shirt-and-drawers philosophy. I've also had sixteen trout for breakfast, but that was also because it was all I had. The worst thing is to eat corned beef and no water. It takes water to hydrolyze that stuff.

"But normally I do very well. Even in a six-inch snow, I can get vegetables out of my garden. I've gone out and pulled brussel sprouts a week after Christmas. The weather gets warmer all the time. Some winters now the temperature never gets lower than ten above. And here, where I've put my garden, even the fairly delicate plants live longer in the fall because the sun comes out late from behind that hill in the morning and doesn't draw out the frost as fast."

Buckskin was soon to demonstrate just how well he can live. After breakfast, he picked up an old wicker backpack and we scuffed through the sand to his rowboat. Bailing out a foot of water in the boat, we shoved off and headed upstream along the shore. At what Sylvan judged a safe distance, we suddenly swung out into the swift current and rowed hard. But hardly in unison. I was reminded that a college coach had not thought much of me as a crew prospect. Despite distinct lack of synchronization, we arrived safely at the little beach on the opposite side and were not swept downstream into the rapids. Several inches of water trickled ominously into the bottom of the boat just during this brief passage.

Walking up the trail, again sampling raspberries and currants, we approached the old Painter mine. The large mill building had fallen down, but the bunkhouse was entirely intact. Through gaping doors and windows, bits of furnishings could still be seen. Peach, pear, and apple trees stood 'round about, and over the shingled roof spread the most magnificent cherry tree one could hope to see anywhere. Huge white Queen Anne cherries clustered along its

96

branches thicker than grapes on any vine. Hundreds and thousands of cherries on this one tree virtually hid the green leaves from sight.

Picking up the long wooden tongue, we pulled an old weathered wagon, whose ancient bearings moved surprisingly easily, under this tree as laden with fruit as a seed catalog cover. Standing in the wagon bed, in the cool shade of the leafy greenness, eating half as many cherries as went into the wicker pack, we picked and picked. Soon we stopped picking bunches of cherries and began pulling off great handfuls, double handfuls, of the pink-tinged, ivory-yellow fruit. Sometimes we ate the bright crimson unripe cherries, which were almost better.

Just one bough busied us for a long time. We finally abandoned it merely because we could no longer pick double handfuls from it, and chose another, moving the squeaking wagon. This we had not half unburdened before our big pack was full, and we headed home.

For some reason, we had little more than tea for lunch. Sylvan, having spent such a hard and unpleasant morning barely surviving in the wilderness, got philosophical again. "People from Manhattan, say," he began, "don't see how anyone could learn and do and make all the things I do. What they don't realize is that in New York, where it's so hard just to live, all their energy is spent trying to exist. Then they hurry and rush all the really important things.

"When I'm finished making a gun, for instance, I set it back aside for a day just to show I'm not anxious how it'll turn out. I may not test it or fire it for weeks. That's what the city does to people. They're so anxious to complete anything that they never plan it out properly or enjoy it right when it's finished.

"People in classical days did a better job of thinking. They were closer to realities. Had a few things against them, though. They had slaves to make 'em lazy."

Sylvan stopped talking. It had become hot. The summer sun had climbed noon high. Heat waves rose from the rocks.

A thermometer registered 104 degrees. A large horsefly droned briefly. Nothing further was said. The halt might have seemed sudden, abrupt, had it not been so natural. Here it was only part of the cyclical course of a day. We sat wordlessly, and without need of words, surveying surroundings whitewashed with light and fervent heat.

Silence, an almost palpable quantity, had settled down—the protracted, unbroken silence of the frontier. It was like this, this midday spell, long ago in the staging stations and outpost forts and squared adobe towns of the old West. Man whittled in warmly hay-scented livery stables, stared stolidly out at the vibrating, on-rolling tablelands from smoky oaken day coaches, from under brims of derby hats, sprawled watching diffident shrunken creeks trickle by from under the shade of cottonwood trees. Somewhere in Kansas Territory a Barlow & Sanderson stage jounced interminably in and out of wheel ruts, its swaying passengers silent as this. Stranger or kith and kin, they have talked out what they have to say, at least for the while, and the incandescent sun discourages idle chatter. So they ride on mute, one insignificant cloud of dust, clatter of wheels, creak of leather in the still, silent, simmering prairie.

Perhaps two hours later, the silence breaks. A word or a slight shift in a seat, and talk resumes, usually unhurriedly, as if the pause had been merely momentary. The sun has lowered, projecting forward shadows from the now jogging horses, and a wisp of a breeze curls into the coach. Conversation quickens as the stage stop comes nearer, turning into real animation as the driver lifts his horn to his lips to sound notice of arrival to the stationkeeper.

So it was at Five Mile. Sylvan drew a book toward him and found his place. I picked another and stretched out on my sleeping bag on the balcony. A lazy boyhood summer afternoon revisited.

When the wind had revived enough to again rustle leaves, Buckskin put down his book and called, "Would you like to swim?" Affirmative. He delved into a chest and

98

produced two suspendered bathing suits cut down from condemned overalls. Making fast time barefooted across the hot sand, we splashed into the frosty-cold river. No sunbather, Sylvan. His pallid skin was lit white against the deep green water by the harsh bright light. With his beard, he looked a lot like the troll under the bridge in the old children's story.

Running back for a towel and drying briskly, we felt clear-headed and enlivened. No sauna bath and subsequent somersault through the snow could have been more effective.

Sylvan was soon back at work. "This pan," he said, indicating the copper vessel in which he was peeling and chopping rutabagas, "would have been worth plenty in the old days because you could put mercury on it and make cleanups." His thoughts directed again to the gold placering past, he showed a number of artifacts of the period, including an old Chinaman's gold pan. "There was a robbery down here at Florence, and they caught the robbers but never found the gold. As much of it as the thieves had, they couldn't have carried it far. That mystery has never been solved.

"Henry Plummer operated, as you know, in Elk City for a while. No, the abandoned Plummer ranch on Sheep Creek isn't connected with him. He kept up a front as a respectable businessman, but he wasn't too careful."

That brought up the Idaho version of the vigilantes whose formation Plummer seemed to inspire wherever he went. He had known a woman related to the vigilantes, Hart recollected, who freely admitted later that those deadly letters signed "XX" or "77" or simply "The Vigilance Committee" had probably signaled the death of a few men who weren't guilty. "But a friend of mine always said that if you found a man shot, chances were he probably needed shooting or you wouldn't have found him in that condition in the first place."

This typically Western lack of concern about the manner of dying of a man known to deserve death suggested to me the story of one of the most enigmatic, most romantic, more recent and least known of all the authentic gunmen-folk-hero-villains. Tom Horn, a handsome chap with penetrating eyes, Roman nose, determined chin, and receding hairline, was hanged at Cheyenne in 1903 for the murder of thirteen-year-old Willie Nickell. The circumstances lead oldtimers who know the story to argue his guilt or innocence to this day, and about no other hired gun of frontier days is there more puzzlement as to whether he should be mustered among the badmen or the good. I decided to tell Sylvan what I considered to be original and accurate elements of the following fascinating tale that I had picked up elsewhere from a variety of sources.

Mary Faler, an aged Indian-looking woman who had supplied me horses and materiel for a packtrip into the Bridger Wilderness of the Wind Range some time ago, first got me intrigued with Horn. Her father, one time sheriff of Pinedale, Wyoming, before he rode off to Hollywood to star in silent movies, had been good friends with Horn, whom she remembers fondly. "He may have been bad, like they say," Mary concedes doubtfully, "but he was sure good to little kids. I knew him when I was just a button. I was his pet, and he called me Boots. He used to take me on his lap and sing 'The Prettiest Flower of the Wildwood.'"

"They caught Horn for killing sheepmen around here once," said George Dowling, a grizzled old wrangler with the tag of a sack of Bull Durham tobacco perpetually hanging out of the pocket of his shirt. "Sheriff Homer Paine rode him off in the back of a wagon with five or six guys pointing guns at him. They hung him too, with a harness on. There was too much money behind him to hang him for real. They say a big rancher up here named Fayette went broke paying to keep Tom Horn from being hung."

Horn started out, at least, on the side of the law. During a notable career as a scout in Arizona and New Mexico Indian wars, he fought against Geronimo. It was Horn's record as Indian scout and stock detective that recommended him to the Wyoming Stock Growers Association (still a thriving institution) when, around 1895, it appointed a secret committee to see what could be done about rustlers. For bounties ranging from $500 to $700, the committee proposed to Horn, he might be able to reproach rustlers for their sins more forcefully and permanently than the tedious processes of law.

Job lots of men began showing up dead, dry-gulched. Always, they had a rock placed under their heads. This was said to be Horn's trademark, proof to his employers that he had done the killing. Soon there began to be victims whose credentials as rustlers were not well established. The chairman of the committee, Senator Joseph Carey, was said to have had second thoughts.

When Levi Powell and a man named Lewis were murdered, Horn was first implicated in the killings. The six-year-old son of Powell identified Horn as the man who had shot his father. In 1900 one Matt Rush, suspected of rustling, was murdered. The posse tracking the killer came upon Horn, and a posseman badly wounded him in the neck, but evidence was again weak.

In July of the first year of this century, in a western Wyoming still very much of the frontier, came the death that ended Horn's career. Willie Nickell, thirteen-year-old son of Kels Nickell, first man to introduce sheep into the Iron Mountain district, was shot dead by a person unknown. Apparently, Willie had been mistaken for his father. Suspicion at first fell on neighbors, the James Millers, who had quarreled with Nickell. However, a convincing alibi by the little Eastern schoolmarm, Glendolene Kimmel, then living at the Nickell place, seemed to absolve them. Ironically, Horn also testified in the Millers' behalf. Throughout the trial—and here the subplots begin to appear—the handsome gunman was seen to be very attentive to the plain young schoolteacher.

Some time later, engaged in a drinking bout in a Cheyenne saloon, Horn was subtly questioned by Joe LeFous, a deputy U.S. marshall. Led to the supposed privacy of LeFous's office, Horn apparently became drunkenly boastful. Or so witnesses said, for LeFous had stationed Deputy Marshall Les Snow and a court stenographer in the next room to listen. Arrest was made in the barroom of the old Inter Ocean Hotel, where Sheriff Ed Smalley simply quietly tapped Horn on the shoulder. Horn could clearly see in the mirror behind the bar that Smalley had the drop on him. Whether or not because of that, he surrendered meekly.

Drama built higher. Autopsy revealed that the bullet killing the Nickell boy had been of much larger caliber than the gun Horn habitually carried, a .30–30. Nevertheless, at a well-attended trial, Horn was sentenced to the gallows. There was an appeal to Governor Chatterton. Glendolene Kimmel, the schoolteacher, weepingly declared she had perjured herself in the Miller trial and said she had heard Miller and one of his sons plotting to kill Nickell. "They will try to lay this on Tom Horn," she quoted Jim Miller as saying, "but he never done it. It was the Millers."

To explain her perjury, Glendolene said, "I felt it would be unfair to punish Victor Miller's son and leave untouched his father and Kels Nickell, the original cause of all the trouble."

Miss Kimmel eventually wrote a booklet to clear Horn's name. It would have been more convincing had it not contained descriptions of Horn as "standing six foot two, broadshouldered, deep-chested, full-hipped . . . without an ounce of superfluous flesh upon him and with muscles of steel. . . ." (Horn also wrote his own account, which I was able to draw on.)

While Chatterton deliberated, Horn sent a letter containing an escape plan to rancher John Coble. Coble's hired men were to dynamite the wall of a corridor where Horn would be exercising. His selected messenger, Hubert Herr, gave the letter to the Cheyenne *Tribune,* and the guard was redoubled.

Eight months later, Horn did escape. In a comic sequence right out of Laurel and Hardy, however, the great escape was marred by his being chased down Nineteenth Street by the middle-aged proprietor of an itinerant merry-go-round who happened to have set up across the street from the courthouse, followed in full hue and cry by a pack of citizens who had just emerged from a Sunday morning church service and had been attracted by the excitement. Horn finally stopped when two bullets hit disconcertingly near him. He never fired his own gun. Why? Because the safety had not released. Merry-go-round proprietor Eldrich confidently and proudly covered the reclaimed prisoner until gendarmes arrived, blissfully unaware that his cheap pistol was now empty. Thereafter the courthouse was guarded by two full companies of militia.

Somber overtones of folk-tragedy redominated on the solemn day that Tom Horn walked up the traditional thirteen steps to the new gallows platform, still redolent of fresh-sawn pine. One could almost have heard, in the mind's ear, an ominous obbligato of doom. "Ed," Horn said, addressing Sheriff Smalley and smiling down at the nervous, slightly green-faced bunch of peace officers gathered below to witness the execution, "that's the sickest lot of damned sheriffs I ever seen."

At Horn's request, two of his friends sang that quaintest of American folk-hymns, "Life Is Like a Mountain Railroad." (I have heard that old hymn sung on one of the last wistful little yellow-painted narrow gauge trains to rock and squeal over the Continental Divide from Durango to Alamosa, Colorado, and it sent shivers down my spine. Idaho oldtimers say such chills mean that someone somewhere is walking over the ground where your grave will be. In this case, where Tom Horn's grave is?)

Then Horn was lifted onto the trap triggering the drop. But the new patent gallows was so complicated that the assembled officials had to watch, in growing unease, for thirty-one seconds until Horn finally swung. Rumors of a bold, last-minute rescue flashed through many minds. After the drop, Horn took seventeen long minutes to die. Before the last moment, one man broke through the police line holding out the public. It was Kels Nickell. Dry-eyed, hating, he surveyed the blue-faced corpse. Nickell had come to make certain that the man hanging there was truly Tom Horn.

After hearing me out, Buckskin, himself well acquainted with the odd, recondite story of Tom Horn, cited plausible reasons for believing Horn not guilty of the Nickell killing. His associates and fellows just got tired of him, Bill thought, and then he *had* killed a lot of people. Besides, "he got to thinking he was God along toward the last."

Horn's undisputable qualifications as an Indian scout reminded Bill to share a number of his own observations on redskins. For example: "When Scotsmen met Indians— most of the Hudson Bay Company men were Scots—the Indian went all to hell, but it improved the Scotsman. And that would be worth almost any sacrifice."

While extolling Col. Richard Dodge's *Thirty-Three Years Among the Indians* as the only really authentic book on the subject, Sylvan got mad all over again just thinking about some of the pretentiously inexpert volumes on Western lore he had read. The book that irritated his sensibilities the most was one that had had its hero shoot a trophy elk, which he then slung over his saddle to pack out. Hart questioned whether anyone, however manly, could so blithely sling around a 1100-pound elk: "This guy's been so busy going to teas where they serve vanilla wafers, he's never had a chance to get west of Ohio or even look at an elk in a zoo."

No such unauthenticity mars Sylvan's perceptions, for the good and simple reason that no Hart—and he in particular—has ever been far enough from the frontier to lose much familiarity with it. Sylvan himself lived in a dugout with a board roof in Indian Territory recently turned Oklahoma. Although he postdated that period, his family had

104

been in the Territory since the great Battle of Adobe Walls, sometimes called Adobe Wells. He still remembers his parents telling him how for weeks eighteen men and one woman held off 5000 Comanches under the half-breed chief Quanna Parker. He remembers how Parker, in a later, more forgiving era, went to Washington and visited President Theodore Roosevelt. The President lectured the chief on his polygamous ways, advising him he ought to keep only one squaw and tell the others to go home. Parker pondered the suggestion just long enough to be struck by the practical problems. *"You* tell 'um," he said.

He remembers how old settlers' store-bought supplies consisted solely of a sack of salt, some flour, and possibly some coffee and a small quantity of sugar; how they would pick wild plums for fruit; how a sack of corn meal or a cow were definite luxuries; how, even then, many and many a pioneer meal would be nothing but corn-meal mush and milk.

The first dwellings were simply brush arbors laid over a pole, maybe with a patch of canvas over the bed to keep that one particular place dry. Potable water was a problem. Sylvan often transported two great fifty-five-gallon oak barrels to the nearest springs to get the family supply. Later, in more established and prosperous times, cisterns were built. These collected rain pouring off roofs, and he remembers vividly how the rainwater tasted of cedar shingles. Picking up a pencil and drawing a picture of such a cistern, Hart first sketched the winch and little buckets on a continuous rope. Then, explaining that these were just as much a part of any cistern, he whimsically drew in a frog and a bug at the bottom.

Nostalgically, Hart spoke of the many cider presses, which were constituted of little more than a wheel, a screw, and a couple of boards. The apples were put into a sack before being pressed to keep most of the seeds and pulp from getting into the cider. He reminded me that saintly Johnny Appleseed, whose real name was John Amos Chapman, got his seeds from just such cider mills back in the earlier Midwest and remarked that Johnny often built fences around his tree plantings to keep off marauding bears, the bane of his life.

Sylvan's only objection to some of the early Indian-Territory improvisings was their lack of elegance—inelegance as meant by the mathematician, who thus scorns any method that does not work most easily and simply. Which is exactly Sylvan's biggest objection to urbanized, over-mechanized, "modern" ways of doing things. "Everything in cities," he says, "has a catch to it: an awful lot of work. All those streets have to be swept and cleaned, all those women have to be taken to beauty parlors and be boiled and pickled and scissored."

All that useless work and striving, Bill thought, was what rotted out the self-reliance, courage, and strength of will of city people. "During that New York blackout, a few soldiers could have lined up people for a crematorium and they'd have gone," he said. "If a few had protested or asked where they were going, they could have yelled at them in a real mean authoritative tone of voice—'You there, *you!* Get back in line!'—prodded them with a bayonet a couple of times. They'd go along then, meek and senseless as lambs.

"Of course, I believe work is good for you. Unless you work pretty hard you'll never be healthy. If you can't discipline yourself, don't worry about your future. You don't have any. But I work only when I want to or need to. Seldom during the hot part of the day, for example. Why, I don't even eat until the sun goes behind that hill.

"There's no job too lowdown that I couldn't do it. Not even cleaning those city streets. I could always learn something from any job. But that might not be a virtue. There's such a thing as being too adaptable, except maybe when you're in a jam, like a war. Why limit yourself to something that'll kill your mind when the world's a whole storehouse of possibilities?"

During a pause in Buckskin's defense of immoderate lib-

106

erty, I wandered to the front gate to look up the river in the fading light. A hen grouse and her brood, who had been strolling up Bill's firewall, froze. I told Bill to come look at this. There the fool-hen and her three chicks stood, straight and stiff as if stuffed and mounted in a museum diorama, not two yards from us. Fascinating. They were close enough so we could count their feathers and see every detail of their seemingly predominantly gray but actually variously tinted coloring. We left them for a while, then returned, perhaps fifteen minutes later. They still stood immobile, all in a straight row just as I had first seen them.

"It's strange, but they always circle this wall counter-clockwise, never clockwise," Sylvan said, his voice causing not even a flicker in the birds' eyelids. "Now here's a creature totally unadapted to anything but life in the wild. They can hardly be raised in captivity. For one thing, they can only eat live, moving food. I've tried feeding them oatmeal. They see it as you drop it, but can't when it stops falling. More important, when they're confined in a closed space, they're killed by their own droppings."

«« 9

Aᴍᴇʀɪᴄᴀ ɪɴ 1969 is twice as close in time, and very likely in spirit also, to the twenty-first century, as to the mythologized but dimly remembered frontier. Yet, although a baby born this hour will first be able to drive a car in that portentous year, 1984, the West that shaped the spirit and purpose of this nation is not totally vanished. What remains continues to shape and recreate the minds of Americans.

An essential article of American faith is the existence somewhere of open lands vast enough to house the American spirit and grand enough to sustain American aspirations. In some unreconstructed, unasphalted places, we need to believe, a little-known canyon, three times as deep as the Empire State Building is tall, drives a miles-long wedge into the western highlands. From the floor of the gorge a symmetrical Gothic spire hewn of free-standing granite strains two thousand feet through the canyon's long twilight toward the narrow streak of white-blue sky above. Roaring between sparkling, mineral-encrusted walls, a black, rushing river carves its way down from timberline's August snowbanks. A waterfall of liquid crystal pitches dizzyingly down the sheer walls.

In such a place it would be possible to turn one's back toward the East, look into the aquamarine shadows of late afternoon, and see wraithlike forms dancing forgotten aboriginal rites beneath the granite spires. A Spaniard curses fearfully at the black gateway to Hades that has suddenly opened up before him; the muted slap of a canoe paddle is drowned by the roaring stream, and an exploring padre prays fervently; a man named Clark or Frémont feels the cold wind from the awesome chasm of a side canyon on his face; surveyors for a transcontinental railroad tramp through, oblivious to Indian massacre, and turn back daunted by the grinding gorge; the haunting wail of a little teakettle of a narrow-gauge locomotive bound for some gold-surfeited ghost town echoes shrilly through the canyon; and then silence returns, disturbed only by the leaping trout.

Salmon River is still just such a place. It still exists, even in the troubled, crowded world of 1969. Others—the Black Canyon of the Gunnison, Clear Creek, Marble Canyon—do not, blotted out by blank sheets of dammed-up water or by multi-lane superhighways.

Yet this summer's hot sun will once again distill an aroma of spices from the Salmon canyon's sheltered vegetation to be borne along the gorge by the speeding river's cool breezes. A walker beneath the towering blue, white, pink, gray, red, and black canyon walls and amid the bright colors of this autumn will still find splashed against a dark background of pine and blue-green spruce the flaming red of scrub oak and mountain mahogany, the bright green of holly-like Oregon grape, and the lemon yellow of aspen and willows. He will find fledgling grouse behaving as foolishly as always, and Sylvan Hart laughing at their buffooneries.

If the visitor is polite and attentive, this kindly, gray-haired man with peaked hidehelmet hat on his balding head will gladly tell how Captain William Clark entered the canyon at present-day North Fork, followed it downstream in rising awe, and was assured by a friendly Indian that he hadn't seen nothin' yet: ". . . those rapids which I had Seen he said was small & trifleing in comparison to the rocks & rapids below, at no great distance & The Hills or mountains were not like those I had Seen but like the Side of a tree Streight up." Hostile Blackfeet acted more subdued after a Scot trapper employer by the Hudson's Bay Company roasted on troublesome brave over his campfire, but the river remained untamed. Four of John Work's Hudson Bay men started down the canyon in 1832. Months later, rescued by Nez Percé, two emerged as the first whites to traverse the gorge. The other two simply vanished from sight at a bend in the river, and all their companions ever found of them or their skin canoe were their paddles.

Hart will tell how the gold rush brought 10,000 men to Florence alone in 1861 and 1862 and how there are not that many people today in all the Salmon River basin. He will tell how prospectors attending the rushes of 1897 and 1902 to Thunder Mountain found precipitated gold even on logs and leaves, and how the ground shook when thunder reverberated off Lightning Peak and Thunder Mountain proper, up there at the head of the South Fork of Holy Terror Creek, and of how whole buildings floated around in the lake that drowned Roosevelt City. There are the stories of how the entire Chinese populations of Leesburg and Loon Creek, grubbing for smaller stakes after the whites had left, were massacred by—depending on whom you asked—either the Sheepeater Indians or renegade whites. And tales of Warren and Leesburg, each divided into feuding towns, named Washington and Richmond in the one case, and Grantsville and Leesburg in the other.

With some encouragement, Hart will retell the story of Hill Beachy and his friend Magruder, probably Idaho's most famed tale of the early years, just as he heard it from men who were alive at the time.

Around 1863, according to Sylvan, Hill Beachy, the famous stagecoach operator whose name ranks near those of Sanderson and Ben Holliday, was running a hotel in Lewiston, Idaho. Lloyd Magruder, his closest friend, operated a trading and freighting business. Late in the summer, Magruder led a sixty-mule packtrain loaded with supplies east to thriving Virginia City, Montana, 325 miles east via Elk City, the old Nez Percé Trail, the Big Hole, and the Ruby Valley. After reaching the Salmon River country, several days later, he was met by a group of eight strangers, also coming from the west. Since they "seemed to be jolly good fellows," Magruder accepted their offer to help with packing in exchange for food. On arrival at Alder Gulch, four of the men left to go prospecting and four—D. C. Lowry, David Howard, James Romain, and William Page —remained in his employ.

When Magruder was ready to return in midautumn with over thirty thousand dollars in gold he had received for his goods and packing services, he engaged the same four men and hired four more new ones. The latest four were two men named Phillips and Allen and two young miners, each with $2000 in gold dust, trying to return home to Missouri. By now the first four had gained Magruder's complete confidence. This was unfortunate, for three were patient but vicious road agents. Page, the fourth, a trapper and mountain man, was threatened with death if he did not go along with their conspiracy. When the party camped near a likely spot, a high cliff overlooking a deep gorge back in the remote Salmon basin, one road agent, Lowry, chopped Magruder to death while the others likewise disposed of the four new packers. Taking the five best mules, the highwaymen ran the rest of the stock over the cliff and threw the dead men after them, tied up in blankets. They all wore moccasins in hopes that, in the unlikely event the murders were discovered, they would be blamed on Indians.

Heading west on the only good trail, as Hart's version goes, the murderers expected to ford the Clearwater above Lewiston. But the weather was so cold that the river was full of running ice. Afraid to cross, the badmen had to enter town. Next morning, they took the first stage out, to Walla Walla.

Meanwhile, in Lewiston, Hill Beachy had had a bizarre premonition, a nightmare detailing the robbery and death

112

of his friend. Already worried, he was confirmed in his fears when he saw the same four men who had followed Magruder out of town sneak into Lewiston so furtively and leave so hastily. Before he had a shred of evidence, he persuaded a judge to issue a warrant for the men's arrest and induced the Governor of Idaho, who happened to be in town, to give him "requisitions" on the help of the Governors of Oregon, Washington, and California. When he found Magruder's saddle, left in Lewiston by the fugitives, and talked to packers who had left Virginia after his friend's departure without seeing Magruder on the trail, Beachy swore vengeance.

Tracing the murderers across all of Washington and Oregon and into California far enough to divine that they had headed for San Francisco, Beachy wired the authorities there from Yreka, the nearest point with telegraph lines. The four were arrested and identified. Finally, Page broke down, telling the whole story. Only Beachy's determined pleas saved the outlaws from lynching.

Beachy got the brigands back to Lewiston where there was just one small problem: they had committed the crime under Idaho law. For nine months, from March 3 (the date Idaho became a Territory) to December 7, 1863 (coincidentally, the day before the trial) Idaho had no law and no penal code—partly because the Territory was so new, partly because of preoccupation with the Civil War then raging, and partly because any law was unenforceable. Literally, murder was not a criminal act.

Precisely that one day before the trial, the legislature approved a code. It was admirably brief: "The common law of England, so far as the same is not inconsistent with the provisions of the Constitution of the United States, the Organic Act and laws of this territory, shall be the law of the land of this territory." Under this law, the three road agents were *ex post facto* tried, convicted, and hung. Page was set free, but died very soon thereafter, killed by persons unknown. All four men were dead before the Idaho snows had

113

even melted enough to allow a search for the bodies of their victims.

"Think of it," Sylvan concluded. "Had Beachy not had his strange dream, or had the weather not been so cold, the murderers probably never would have been found."

Once begun, Sylvan can relate many another spectral tale of the Salmon River country, particularly of wicked Florence. He speaks of gamblers Pinkham and Patterson, giant figures who met over faro and monte in Florence in 1862 before their final deadly confrontation at Warm Springs. Bold, chivalric Pinkham, a strong and agile man of over two hundred pounds and six feet, with an habitual frown and steely gray eyes masking a violently intense nature. Pinkham, onetime sheriff and marshal in Boise County, who hired a drummer and fifer on the Fourth of July and followed them, waving the flag of Union through the streets of rebeltown, and no man dared protest. And Patterson, an equally big Tennesseean of fair complexion, his light hair and sandy whiskers streaked with gray, his calm blue eyes sad and reflective—a gentle man turned by whiskey into a raging demon, who once scalped a female acquaintance for some fancied slight.

In Hart's narration, an Indian squaw rides again to Florence and to Warren to warn of Indian uprising. Fat Jack, a grotesquely skeletal outlaw, is driven out of Florence by the Vigilantes into the teeth of a storm. Turned away at every door, freezing in the sleet, Fat Jack is finally taken in by kindly Old Man Neselrode. Night riders riddle both outcast and samaritan host with a score of bullets.

Sylvan talks of notorious Matt Bledsoe ("I'd as soon kill a man as eat breakfast"), who came to town in 1861, and the even more infamous Boone Helm, who arrived in 1862. With a reputation for cannibalism already well established, Helm was known to have said, when asked about the disappearance of a companion, "Why, do you suppose that I'm damned fool enough to starve to death when I can help it? I ate him up, of course." Almost absentmindedly, Helm shot

114

Dutch Fred, who was standing weaponless, arms calmly folded across his chest, in a crowded Florence saloon. A year later, when law enforcement had improved somewhat in town, Boone was brought back, as a sort of afterthought, to stand trial. No witnesses appeared. They had all been bought or frightened off. Helm was released.

Chief of all the outlaws according to Hart, was evil Charley Harper, who ran Florence for two years as an absolute despotism. One of his lieutenants, Brockie, once tried to shoot another named Hickey and missed, killing a bystander. Brockie was tried and found innocent on the grounds that the death was accidental because the shot had missed its intended target. More commonly, trials were not held at all.

Anyone interested, as I was, in pursuing futher the stories that Hart has helped to hand down would relish Nathaniel Langford's *Vigilante Days and Ways,* a classic, definitive, and now rare nineteenth century account of the Idaho and Montana vigilantes, which corroborates many of them. For to Langford, "A meaner, baser, more contemptible band of ruffians perhaps never before disgraced the annals of the race."

Could these have been members of the same princely breed Sylvan describes meeting in the early thirties? Very likely. Danger, raw wealth, and distance from artificial, imposed law have always both attracted and produced men of extremes. The very good and the very bad warred constantly—often, as examination of the reality in the myths of the badmen will reveal, within the same person. Because of its fragility, human life was both precious and cheap. The unspeakable beauty and boundless bounty of the wilderness enlarged many a man; its harshness brutalized many another.

Joaquin Miller, a poet of the California gold rush, a practicing miner and diarist of the Idaho boom, very nearly echoes Sylvan's phrases. "There is a sort of Freemasonry among miners and all sorts of honest men of the gold mines," he wrote. "They have been a sort of civilized advance army. There are men who have stepped to the front from out of millions. . . . You can always find more sincere manhood and real politeness in a mining camp with its sprinkling of cattlemen, grangers, and the like than in . . . London and Paris."

Transfixed by the unearthly splendor of the Rockies in the secret places I will show to only a few, I have very often thought to myself that those who live always amid such grandeur should find it impossible to live as meanly as other men. One can walk or even drive through these opalescent lands and feel their force, but it is perhaps best of all to traverse them as did the pioneers, on horseback. It is astonishing, really, how quickly one falls into the rhythm and routine of a previous century. Time and space very soon reassume their natural proportions, and within a day or two it seems only normal to rise at first warmth of dawn, to saddle and to pack, to plan a journey in terms of a handful of miles.

The West is still to be found beyond the Bitterroots and the Sawtooths, if one will only ride those few miles to meet it. The slow winding of a pack train along a tortuous trail, the *plock* and splash of horses' hooves fording a shallow rocky stream, the steady soporific procession across upland meadows as a hot sun dictates removal of garments donned in chill morning, the wheezing and blowing of mounts as riders shift weight forward on a grade—these set the tempo, and the tempo is the 4/4 time of cowboy balladry.

Drop your reins over the pommel; then, as your horses splash into a pothole at afternoon's end, breaking the pool's pale gold transparency, take time to see the archtypical Remington scene of drinking animals and lowering sun.

Soon enough, every evening, that pale gold, along with ink-green pines and white granite rocks turned a pale arctic blue, will be the only colors of the high-country moonscape. Even the tent you have pitched—linen-white, perhaps supplied by a Denver Tent & Awning (est. 1859) , and in all

116

respects first cousin to the shelter of the original mapmakers and prospectors—will be that same watercolor-wash blue. Scramble a hundred feet up the rim of an austere upland bowl campsite, look down toward the flickering orange spot of the campfire, and you see a scene differing in no detail from a hundred-year-old glass-negative photograph by Charles R. Savage or William Henry Jackson.

Descriptions can never convey adequately the extravagant lavenders and cobalt blues of the sunset, or the quintessentially lonely beauty of the untouched land. They could never convey how a haunted river remains just as it was, amid the box canyons and jack-o'-lantern buttes, when a forgotten branch of the Oregon Trail wound along its crooked, deep-carved banks. Nor how, as far as the eye sees in any direction, the parapeted mesas and silver sage are unchanged not only from the time of the Trails, but from long before. Were it not for occasional wheel ruts cut into sandstone, the river itself would forget whether the creak of wagons, the crack of canvas in the wind, the snuffling of oxen were memories of the past or premonitions of the future.

10

ONE FINE MORNING we rose early to prospect for gold and other treasures. Something about watching the rose-fingered dawn touch the wine-dark river made me ask Hart what was the latest he had ever slept in during his thirty-three years in the wilderness. Sylvan pondered judiciously. "Seven o'clock," he said. (It must be nice, I thought, to live for thirty-three continuous years in a place so full of pleasant things to do and see that you can't abide staying in bed a minute longer than necessary.) "I got up at four o'clock for a while in college to study Greek," Sylvan added. "You can see what a bad character I'd be around people." He winked broadly. "I'd get up some mornings at four to study Greek, other mornings I'd be hammering on copper, and then sometimes I'd have to shoot a little. Not just every set of neighbors would like that very well."

Buckskin, after some more fried squash for breakfast, selected a big California-style gold pan and tucked it under his arm. We began our quest for riches. Picking up and hefting a small piece of spotted rock, Bill said, "This should be a good piece of quartz. It's highly mineralized and those little bug-holes should contain gold." After grinding the rock to powder with a huge, ancient cast-iron mortar and pestle used for that purpose in the old days, he swept the rock dust into the gold pan and walked down to the river.

Dipping up some water, he began panning. After deftly washing off the light dust and rust with a gentle sluicing action of the water, Sylvan swirled out the remaining heavier dust all over the bottom of the pan with one expert flick of his wrists. Suddenly, there in the thin layer of black, a whole streak of gold lay exposed.

Suddenly, all California was in that pan. The cascade of tiny bits of gold reflected visions of the American River and Hangtown, Bannack and Alder Gulch, Ophir and Cripple Creek, Samarkand and Golconda. One second before, this had been dull dust, a mere exercise in mineralogy. Now it was exciting. How can plain crushed rock and metal be exciting? But it is, and always has been. Some very primitive lust or greed does brush, cobweblike, across the darker recesses of the brain at the sight of raw free gold.

"There may be two thousand pieces of gold there," Sylvan said, smiling, "yet it's only a few pennies' worth, because it's so fine. There's monazite, a scarce compound containing the rare earths cerium and lanthanum, arsenic and platinum, too. But there's gold enough so that it's a real yellow color."

We began walking up the river. "Prospecting is like fishing," Sylvan said. "You usually feel you're on the wrong side of the river." He waved his arm toward a trough-like depression and explained it was where he had had his sluice box when placering. Appropriately for the Salmon River country, our search for a likely spot to find gold was not a long one. Picking out a tiny sandy hollow in the bank not far upstream, Hart began scooping up sand from beneath the shallow water, digging down to rock level to get a panful of the kind of yellow-tinged brown stuff he wanted. (Gold, being so heavy an element, always settles to bedrock in a river.) Again he began that gentle circular sluicing motion. Again that fringe of black sand emerged at the top of the tilted pan.

"That's magnetite," Bill said. "The gold is down there with that." Hunkered down on two rocks by the edge of the

120

river, just as easy and comfortable as if he were sitting on a parlor sofa, Buckskin continued swirling. This time, as the light-colored sand washed off, it left behind a great deal of black. "Look at all that black sand," Buckskin said. "That would indicate a lot of gold, except instinct tells me I didn't dig deep enough."

Again Bill finished off his panning with a wrist-flick, spreading out the color over the magnetite. "By gosh, this is at least a nickel's worth," he said. "Look at that one big color, and it's just lousy with smaller ones." True enough, there were now definite little pieces of gold.

"A lot of this was put in just the last two months, during the last high water," Sylvan declared. "The river's been mining and milling and depositing this gold for that time."

Although Hart had started this panning session merely as a mechanical demonstration of technique, now an old prospector's interest flickered briefly: the river had demonstrated that panning it might just barely pay. Sylvan estimated that a man might make five dollars a day. That sounded moderately good until he explained his calculation. At five cents per pan, allowing six minutes for each and swirling the heavy pan steadily all day in the cold water, he would have to work rapidly for ten full hours to earn his five dollars.

Observing my diminished enthusiasm for this way of making a living, Buckskin pointed out that during the thirties men settled for ten cents a day if panning or a dollar a day if they had invested effort in building a sluice box. He particularly remembered a man named Andy Strausser who had done just that for quite some time. Strausser could— and did—pack in all his supplies for an entire year on one horse, and at that they consisted mostly of oatmeal and cracked wheat. Practically the only exception was one fifteen-cent can of cocoa, for celebrations.

Knowing that gold was separated from sand and other minerals by amalgamating it with mercury, I asked Hart how he would retrieve the gold from the amalgam. He replied that a prospector would often squeeze the amalgam through a piece of sheepskin. Because of fluidity, mercury would pass through the skin, leaving the gold behind. If the prospector had only a little bit of gold—an ounce or so—he might likely hollow out a potato, put in the amalgam, and bake the whole thing in his campfire. When the potato was removed from the fire, thoroughly baked, the mercury would be on top of the hollow in the potato and the gold would be on the bottom.

Those long wooden sluice boxes, usually fed water by still longer wood flumes snaking down over the semiarid hillsides from some higher creek, have always seemed to me one of the most fascinating artifacts of gold placer mining. Now, unlike the gold pan, they are disappeared forever, displaced first by hydraulic hosing and then by the almost equally disfiguring dredges of the thirties. They exist only in faded photographs of the California 1850s and in occasional television reruns of movies like Gary Cooper's and Maria Schell's *The Hanging Tree*. But Sylvan still knows how to make them and actually used them in his early days on the Salmon River. From personal experience, Hart recommends that cotton blanket with a pronounced nap be placed at the bottom of the square, U-shaped sluice box. Over that should be put burlap; over the burlap, onion sacks; over the onion sacking, a sharp-edged metal lath to cut up the clay. You will need twenty to thirty feet of box, slanted at about a thirty degree angle or maybe a little less, depending on the consistency of the muck you are shoveling into the sluice. The incline should be just gradually sharpened enough so that the stuff washes thoroughly. If this is done right, the finer and heavier material—the gold—will sink to the bottom, the rocks and pebbles will stay on top, and extraneous dirt will simply wash right down off the sluice. Most of the gold will settle into the blanket. To clean up, you wash the blanket in a tub, pour in a double amount of mercury, and pan the resulting amalgam.

Buckskin was slightly scornful of the early primitive

method of merely tacking occasional sharp metal strips over wool blanketing and also of the rocker method of placering, which he correctly characterized as a crude expedient useful only when the gold was plentiful enough to waste. Of course, rockers *were* handy for extracting gold more rapidly than you could with a pan, without investing the time and effort needed to build a sluice. Basically, they were limited to situations where there was too much gold to pan and too little to construct sluice boxes and flumes.

Thus qualifying his interest in the technique, Hart sketched a diagram to show how one might chop a rocker from a log with an ax. The finished rocker was shaped like an inverted V with a handle. On top was stretched a big grizzly (coarse screening) and midway down a small grizzly (finer-mesh screen, placed at a less steep angle). Gold-bearing material would be spooned in with what amounted to a large ladle.

Hart's easy familiarity with placer mining draws that now all but forgotten art out of the past into the present. The poet Joaquin Miller, writing of this very valley, once asked the question: "Do you know the music of the pick and shovel as they clang and ring on the bedrock, the rattle and the ring of the sluice fork in the hands of the happy, tall, slim man who stands astride the sluice and slings the gravel behind him in high heaps of polished pebbles?" Sylvan Hart, for one, can still answer it, yes.

". . . . for half a year no one touched the bars of Salmon River," Miller continued, in his 1894 *Illustrated History of Montana.* "They yielded richly, however, when once opened. Never anywhere on the face of the earth was gold found to be so plentiful and accessible. Dwarf pines of the Douglas class stood so thick on the hills all about that a horse could not pass through a grove of them; but in the shallow gulches only grass grew. This grass had thirsty, matted roots which ran down to a thin stratum of decomposed quartz. In this lay the grains of gold, as thick in places as wheat on a threshing floor; and indeed it was about the size and color of wheat." Here, in the sluicing Salmon River, Sylvan still prospects.

Did I know that there was an arrastra near here, Bill asked? Its remains were still quite visible and we should hike down to see them. Good, I said, getting enthusiastic about seeing an example of the very earliest means of milling gold ore, the method employed by the first Spaniards and by Coronado in his search for the mythical Indian cities of Cibolla and Quivira. We set off immediately, passing on the way the bleached skeleton of a long-deceased elk and the site of Buckskin's first brush shelter near Five Mile. Bill paused to tell how, after living one summer in a willow tepee at Mackay Bar, he came to this place and slept in a trench with boughs over it. One could just barely see where the trench had been, strategically located between the fire and a heat-reflecting, windbreaking rock. "If you need quick shelter," he said, "the best of all is a fallen tree, right in the hole where it's uprooted itself. You already have half a dugout."

Buck recalled that he lived here when he was still placering full-time with another man. "We sent samples to his old man, who was an assayer," he said. "They kept coming back negative. Finally we sent him a real rich one to see if he could really assay. 'Traces of gold,' he sent back. 'Why, you SOB,' his son wrote him, 'if you had a mine like that, you'd be rich.'" He probably just wanted his son back home to help mind the store.

A couple of rocky, undulating miles of path upstream from Bill's camp, we reached the Little Fivemile, in whose gulch the arrastra was set. Sure enough, the circular stone base could be made out easily. The grinding stones lay there yet, and in each one could be seen the drilled hole in which an iron ring had been seated. The chains attaching the rings to the spokes of the arrastra had long since been diverted to other uses, as had the spokes themselves, but the timber joints of the center hub or axis still remained. One could almost see the yoked ox which had once plodded

124

around and around the perimeter, dragging the heavy stones over the ore to crush it.

After drawing his impression of an arrastra, Bill threw in a stamp mill for good measure, clearly illustrating how its steam- or water-revolved eccentric wheel lifted the huge stamp and then let it come crashing down onto the ore below. Satisfied by his artistry, he returned to pointing out relics. Here was the log frame of the arrastra owner's old camp, there an old placering machine used in later years.

Sylvan had started walking around in tight little circles down on the stony beach a few yards below. "I found an Indian horse hobble down here not so long ago," he said, his head down and looking and staring intently at the ground. He gestured toward a big flat rock. "An Indian sat on that rock and made arrah heads. You can still find chips and spoiled heads. Aha!"

Hart bent quickly and came up brandishing a stone that looked like any other stone on the beach. He claimed it was an Indian fist hatchet. It was still just another rock to me until I hefted it in my own hand. Than I could feel the perfect weight and balance, could touch the slight indentation for the fingers, and could see the once-sharp cutting edge worn round by use and by erosion in the high waters of the Salmon River. Just as easily, Sylvan picked up another, and then an arrowhead.

All the way back to his compound, Hart talked about ancient Indian weapons and tools. When we sat down at his table again, he brought out a large boxful of such artifacts he had found in this country and also in Oklahoma. He showed arrowheads of all varieties, thumb scrapers, awls, knives, and the so-called bird points—small, almost miniature arrowheads. "A lot of people think these were used to shoot birds," he said, "but they weren't. They were attached to a light, short shaft which was in turn attached to a heavy one. That way the whole arrah penetrated farther." His knowledge of this point fascinated me, for even museums sometimes make the "bird point" mistake.

But Buckskin had better treasures. He pulled out a long agate drill, found in an ancient Indian cave, and a collection of beads, all blue. "Some of the first traders nearly starved to death because they brought too many red or green beads with them," he said, "and the Indians only wanted blue. These were made by the Indians themselves, and as you can see they're all different shades and all blue." He also had pottery fragments, including one with a design formed by tying string around the wet clay.

And then he had several arrowheads made from exotic materials. "In later years, Indians made arrowheads from beer bottles and frying pans," he explained earnestly. Then that sly, crafty expression stole over his face again, and he tossed a steel arrowhead onto the tabletop. "This is the one that came out of my operation," he said. Onto the shiny steel was engraved neatly, *Greetings paleface*.

"I have some spearheads, too," Sylvan said, exhibiting some. "The reason spearheads are all old and rare is that the Indians didn't need them. It was only in the period when they had really big game, like mammoths, that they used spears." Among Sylvan's samples, chipped from obsidian and quartzite, were a recognizable Cascade and an intriguing modified point resembling the rare and beautiful Folsom.

From his study of the cave in which he found his 2000-year-old carbon, Hart believes people inhabited the Salmon River canyon 10,000 years ago, with principal campsites near or on his own location. "By the looks of their camp-fires, they were always hungry," he says. "When they got a few mussels, they just about blackened the outsides and loosened the shells before eating them. They didn't wait to marinate anything. There aren't even but a few bones. Either they ate them, or else they cracked them to get the marrow.

"As you see, primarily I'm a student," Hart said now after a moment's silence. "All I need is a place to study and a place to experiment." I asked whether the increasing

126

number of people coming in to visit him, mostly during summer float trips down the Salmon, bothered him or his studies. "I rather like people," Sylvan admitted. "There could be any number here and it wouldn't bother me. When I'm working I like to work uninterruptedly, but when it's too hot to work it isn't necessarily too hot to talk.

"Besides, all the visitors are different. They don't ask the same questions. It's interesting. I can tell what worries a person by what he asks. 'How often do you get mail?' 'What do you do if you get sick?' 'Don't you get lonely?' "

A few of the visitors have been moderately well known. "Well, Lady Bug Johnson hasn't been here, but Ethel Kennedy's hat has," Buckskin said. "It was a straw hat with red roses around the band. She left it somewhere upstream, and someone brought it down here for safekeeping for a while."

Coincidentally, not two hours after this conversation, another pilgrim arrived, a woman who had visited Hart once before she was married and who was now bringing in a grown daughter and a younger son. It was interesting to see the latent ladies' man in Sylvan emerge. He chatted even more amiably than usual about his experiences as a fire lookout and as an elk skinner, redoubled his output of amusing stories, and flattered his guests outrageously. He chuckled appreciatively as the woman reminded him of the story of a local rancher who was rumored to have shot his wife for having had an affair with the schoolteacher who had been brought in to tutor the children. The rancher had escaped any tiresome troubling by the law because only he and his brother lived in the vicinity. Both Sylvan and the lady facetiously took the moral to be the difficulty of living with a woman on the Salmon River, but to me it could have as easily illuminated the problems of raising children in such remote country.

Buckskin also listened attentively while the woman told of a man who had recently set his house afire with his wife in it. "In Boise they've got women to burn," he said mock-mournfully, "but here we've got hardly any."

127

After the women and children had left, Bill returned to showing a little portable set of gold scales complete with gold values scratched on the backs of the weights [2 dwt (two pennyweight) $= 175$ (for $1.75)] and a magnet to take out any iron the unscrupulous might try to smuggle into the gold. Bill uses the scales to weigh gunpowder. He also demonstrated use of a drilling spoon and drilling steel, with me holding and rotating the drill while he hammered, and wincing only a little. We also examined Hudson Bay trade goods (Bill has a pot with a date of 1856 on it), eggs ("one thing about eggs—if you turn 'em over every month you'll never have a bad one") and analyzed the weather.

Asking Buckskin a question like, "Do you think it will rain?" elicits a more complicated answer than you might suppose. Beginning by decreeing that no, it will not rain because those are ice clouds, Bill will proceed to tell you the equinox is generally preceded by a storm in this country and you are much more likely to have snow on Christmas than not. By the time he is through, you have learned that the beginning of spring can be as early as February 20 and "the only way you can be sure is to hear a woodchuck chirp. If it's a fine, fine day and you don't hear them, you can expect lots more snow."

The sun now plunged down behind the mountains with the surprising speed it exhibits when one is really watching it. Cool shadows crawled up over us. The dark began to gather. As humankind has always done in places wild, remote, and blood-quickening in the hours of dusk, we fell to entertaining ourselves by calling to life the ghosts of the strong and violent men who had inhabited this massive land.

My curiosity piqued by a passing remark of Sylvan's during a previous visit, I had dipped into the strange history and legend of Old Man Bender, just as I had been spurred to investigate other fragments of history by Hart's tales. Perhaps the most satanic of all the Western stories, its set-

128

ting in the pristine America of the frontier only reinforces its gothic horrors.

The version I reported back to Sylvan had Bender (no one ever knew his Christian name) living in Dodge City in vigilante days, days when Dodge was the twilight zone between civilization and savagery, days when Dodge had had a dozen sheriffs and not a live honest one yet. There Bender ran a roadhouse with his daughter Kate, a tall, bowlegged, gangly witch of a wall-eyed girl. Despite her spooky looks, raven-haired Kate was not without certain evilly attractive charms. Many a moneyed guest, it was said, was lured to death in a dark rear room by her lascivious dancing. But if the number of men entering Bender's seedy premises was greater than the number emerging, this after all was Dodge, and no one was keeping a census.

Finally, however, one of Dodge's rare and perishable honest sheriffs grew so brave as to visit the saloon to try to find out why so many of Bender's customers were never seen thereafter. Pretending drunkenness and lust, the sheriff followed cockeyed Kate into the dark. He, too, never emerged.

Next day, the whole saloon was empty and silent. Citizens broke in to investigate. In the infamous back room, they found the sheriff dead on the floor, his head nearly severed from his body. The girl was dead, too, clutching a bloody hatchet, a bullet drilled neatly through her cast eye. In a black moldering cistern under the plank floor, the investigators found eight decomposing corpses, each with a crushed skull.

That much is a slight variant of the standard Bender Tale. It is one of the great true horror stories of the old West. To this day, it is discussed and argued in lonesome cabins and around late-night campfires. In what I had come across in an old book, with considerable excitement, however, there was an eerie sequel.

The scene shifts, many years later, to a desolate stretch

along the Salmon River in Idaho in the gold rush days. A lone miner, traveling between Salmon City and Challis, pursued a runaway pack animal far off the trail into some God-forsaken gulch. There he found a starving, helpless man with hollow cheeks and glazed eyes. Staying with the poor old man for weeks, the miner nursed him back to health. One night, just before they were ready to move on, the stranger, recovered, knocked out the sleeping samaritan's brains with an ax and stole one of his horses.

Sheerly by chance, residents of Salmon happened to discover the murder. Following the murderer's trail, they at length captured him and brought him back into town with the idea of sharing the pleasure of hanging him with the whole community. There he was recognized as Old Man Bender, after all those years still a man with a huge price on his head. Debate raged as to whether to risk taking him all the way to Kansas to claim the reward or to preserve him for the noose.

While making up their minds, they chained the villain to a stake by the ankle, jeered and kicked him, and told him in vivid detail of the fate awaiting him. Cowardly as are most killers, Bender was reduced to sodden blubbering, pleading for his life. But when the miners temporarily adjourned their revenge and returned to their meeting hall to deliberate further vengeance, the old man took out a pocketknife, cut off his chained foot, and set out walking on the bloody stump. Chased by his enraged former captors when they at last discovered the escape, he finally bled to death out in the wilderness.

Cheated of their satisfaction, the Salmon citizens feared losing the reward as well. Since it was summertime, the body could not be shipped the many days' trip back to Kansas without spoiling beyond sure identification. At last an Indian witch doctor said to bury the body in a nearby swamp, where it would keep until winter.

But after interment, the treacherous Indian stole the corpse, dragging it dripping out of the marsh, and after-

130

ward told how one leg jerked spasmodically as he hauled away the body. Attempting to quiet the grim convulsion, the witch doctor buried a tomahawk in the specter's skull. After stewing the corpse in a cauldron to make medicine for his aboriginal gods, the savage laid the bare bones to bleach high in the limbs of a pine tree according to tribal custom.

Years later, a wandering miner found a skull in a pine tree and brought it to town, where, as the story goes, it still lies behind the bar of an old saloon. Plainly visible in its temple is the scar of an ax wound.

That's a lot of action packed into a short script. My experience with unbelievable Western stories has been that for every fiction, invention or excess, you can find—somewhere in frontier history—two or more even more spectacular documentable facts. Even so, I was slightly inclined to doubt this story. The sequel, at least, was just too neatly symmetrical and ingeniously lurid to be credible.

Attracted though he was by the extension of the West's most notorious tale to the Salmon River country, Sylvan strongly agreed with me. "I got the classical tale about the Benders from a teacher back in Nineteen and 'teens," he remembered, "and then I've always been interested because my father and grandfather came from the Benders' section of Kansas, which was not Dodge City—that's a later improvement on the story—but certain vanished towns over in eastern Kansas. I doubt the part about Kate's being such a siren, too. The way I heard it, the Benders would just seat their roadhouse guests with their backs to a sheet hung close to their table. Kate, who was supposed to be fixing food in the back room, could see the victim through the sheet, and she'd just knock him on the head with the ax. A lot of the other sounds like embroidering on the story to make it more gruesome. It didn't need to be any more gruesome. They dug up people from under rocks, trees, and wagon wheels for years after the Benders disappeared. Two men and two women were found in one well.

"The Benders—a lot of low-class slop-bucket Germans—

were spooky enough as it is. Kate would ride a black horse at full speed at night in the thunder, rain, and lightning. The boy, her brother, had a silly eerie laugh, like an idiot or a madman. The old man was probably the strangest of all. If you came in somewhere smoking a cigar, that'd be reason enough to kill you, you see.

"There have been a lot of speculations about what finally became of Bender. Some say Kate killed him. It was a standing cliché in the West for many years to tease any man of about the right age about his being Old Man Bender."

Buckskin grimaced, stroked his chin whiskers, and chuckled drily. "Been a lot of people killed around here, too," he said, squinching his eyes up into a grin, "but I've never been much troubled by ha'nts. Maybe that's because they were such low-grade people they didn't amount to anything as ghosts either.

"An honest ghost should be good for a thousand years," Bill added, tossing a light parcel wrapped in brown paper across the table. "Here. Look at this." Pasted neatly on the package, under a bevy of English postage stamps and an English postmark, was a label with postal instructions. "This package," the label said, "contains the GHOST of the 10th Century bar Maid Harriet whom Ternfull and Witherspoon Ltd. certify as harmless and industrious: value 17/6/ Kind Sirs, you may x-ray this package but do not open lest the contents escape. If you do, I will expect you to recapture mdse. and repack. Please pass this promptly if you can as Old Bill needs this ghost to polish copper."

"Hannah, my nephew Rodney's new wife, sent me that," Buckskin said. "It's not a very valuable ghost, so the antiquities commission let it out of the country."

One small stone clacked a short way down the hillside opposite Buckskin's compound, and we both looked up. Two mountain sheep, ewes, were walking slowly up the faint trail to the salt lick above Bill's place. Little puffs of dust rose from the trail as they walked. One ewe turned away from the other, coughing from the dust, a deep huffing sound like a big bellows—mountain sheep must have very large lungs—followed by a sniffle. Then they both bent to licking the salt. Buckskin pointed out that the one on the right, the one with a horn broken off, was probably pregnant. The mountain sheep lambed the first week in August or the last week in July, he said.

Two more bighorns, and then another, sauntered up the trail. Five of the six local sheep were now in attendance, including one young ram. They stayed as long as we watched them. Some time after we had gotten bored with them and turned to something else, we looked again. Absolutely silently, the bighorns had faded back into the mountains.

«‹‹«‹‹11

BRIGHT AND EARLY next morning I rose, ate more zucchini for breakfast, packed my pack, and rolled up my sleeping bag. Necessarily, I retraced my path to Mackay Bar, to Dixie, to Elk City and Grangeville, largely to learn more about the Bender saga for Sylvan, but also to learn more about the Salmon country itself.

At Grangeville, I stopped at a trailer camp near the mountain of pine logs flanking the sawmill to talk to Jack Taylor, a handsome gray-eyed, graying, ex-Minnesotan friend of Hart's who used to work the Painter mill near Five Mile and live in the old bunkhouse under the Queen Anne cherry tree. "I can remember when I first came in the country," he reflected, "J. R. [Painter] was down there all alone with kerosene boxes and boxes full of ore, and there wasn't a rock you couldn't find free gold on. We crushed it in a ball mill and it went six hundred dollars a ton in a seam ranging up to a couple of feet wide. The water started to come in on us from the river and we had no pumps. Between that and J. R. gettin' in a rag chew with his partners, the mine quit, but that gold is still in there."

From Grangeville, I had decided, I would travel to Salmon City to find out, if I could, whether the famed and grisly Bender saga had indeed reached its climactic end in Idaho. Again the size, ruggedness, and blissful isolation of

135

much of this country asserted itself. From Five Mile Bar to Salmon City is eighty-one miles as the eagle flies (more than 100 as the river runs), but by automobile road it is a far piece—no less than three hundred and ninety miles. For a highway trip, it is rewarding in itself, one of the better in the United States. North down the South Fork of the Clearwater to the atmospheric woods towns of Stites and Kooskia, the views range from narrow canyon to wide and handsome. Turning east at Kooskia, you follow the fertile, well-watered valley of the Middle Fork to Lowell, last outpost of recreational-housing clutter and the junction of the splendid Lochsa and Selway Rivers. The rocky Selway in particular, winding through the Selway Bitterroot Wilderness Area, amply deserves its designation as an official Wild River.

The Army Corps of Engineers has plans for such a choice piece of unstraightened river. The Corps' proposed Penny Cliffs dam would drown both the Selway and the Lochsa, a proposition which would shock by its audacity had not the Engineers diluted its impact by planning to plug virtually every valley in the high mountains.

Untamed and beautiful as is the Selway, the journey up the Lochsa is nearly as interesting, despite the constant proximity of highway to river. Most of the one hundred-odd miles from the Lowell area to the next serious intersecting road, which happens to be way over into Montana, lie in canyon. The effect is much like entering a one hundred-mile-long tunnel or viaduct. All that long way there is nary a gas station, motel, hot dog stand, or even a Burma Shave sign. There is modern highway under wheel (fortunately, lightly traveled) and occasional roadside campgrounds, but on each side silent, impassive wilderness stretches back undisturbed farther than the average city dweller would care to walk in a month. Natural scale and perspective are restored. No longer shrunken, distorted, or overshadowed by busy human beavering, the million details of the landscape loom large, as if magnified. Each creek, with its waterfall tumbling into the Lochsa, becomes a land-

136

mark. Each rare pack trail crossing seems, here, a highroad of commerce. You could no more pass one without noticing it than you could miss an Interstate elsewhere. Your isolated narrow ribbon of automobile modernity comes to seem a strange anomaly, and you peer up each perpendicular gulch to see the real, unanachronistic world. Somewhere up there to the north on the ridgetops, you know, is the ancient Lolo Trail. Long the main Indian route across the Great Divide, it was the path followed by Lewis and Clark on their odyssey to the Pacific and is still little more than a wagon road.

Surmounting the Bitterroot Range at panoramic Lolo Pass and dropping down into Montana, perhaps the state best retaining its native sweeping grandeur, tempts one to explore some of the good ghost towns lurking east and south of the aptly named Sapphire and Garnet Ranges. At first sight of these shining mountains in the slanted light of early morning, I yielded cheerfully. Passing through Missoula in the morning, I overtook the shades of Lewis, Clark & Co. speeding up the Clark Fork at seventy miles per hour to make up in time what was lost in distance.

At Bearmouth, where Bear Creek flows into the Clark Fork and where only a single stage stop stands, one turns left. Some thoughtful soul, blessed with talents for neat lettering and inventive spelling, has put up signs denoting the site of Beartown, once inhabited by 5,000 brawling toughs. North of here the narrow road begins climbing sharply and showing intentions of becoming perfectly villainous. No trip to a ghost town is really good without a really bad road, evil gray skies, hail, wind, and torrential rain threatening to turn to snow or to wash out the grade. Garnet promised to provide all these.

The road never did get too formidable, yet Garnet was no disappointment. It is one of those gratifying ghosts which jump out at you suddenly, at a bend, and which are larger than you had expected. Several falsefronts stand in a little hollow—First Chance Gulch—and a truly satisfying number of sagging cabins dot the hillside. The setting is appropriately high, windswept, and lonesome, even in mid-summer; and the decaying upstairs rooms of the old hotel have windows which frame a quantity of memorably moody views. To watch a storm come up the hill, assault a deserted town with much pounding of hail and soughing of wind, and march down the other side—all from the creaking shelter of a haunted hotel room or the open dripping door-way of a miner's cabin—is to see the essence of some preter-naturally grand Wagnerian opera. After such a storm, birds trill, fragile mountain flowers bloom more translucently bright than ever, and the silent unbidden spectator leaves with all his faculties freighted with sensations.

Down off the mountain, as so often happens, the rain completely disappeared, and I neared Gold Creek, another old boom town 22 miles east, in intense late-afternoon sun-light. Because Gold Creek was mostly a railhead, I headed south, toward the mountains and toward the big old gold town of Pioneer City. Some mountains and some streams just *look* auriferous. If you see enough of them, you learn to sense likely locales for bonanza. This was that kind of excit-ing country, with, I now learned, only one sad lack: Pioneer City has vanished almost without trace. Buckskin has a book with an excellent photograph of Pioneer in its prime. He would be disappointed to learn of its total demise.

But I was right about the mountains, as I discovered when I turned back to Alternate U.S. 10 and took that down along their west edge to Philipsburg and Granite. Entering Philipsburg in the evening, when all such half-deserted cities should be first seen, I found it a little Leadville or Butte or Helena or nineteenth-century Denver, unknown to the outside world but filled with fascinating old build-ings on steep, crooked streets. Like other such places, it has a strange brooding quality, as if a dying town of inanimate brick and stone could remember the wealth and romance that once enlivened its days and nights.

Unlike Philipsburg, which is a city become a village

while retaining city trappings, Granite, the gold town for which P'burg was railhead, supply point, milltown, and cosmopolis, is a true ghost. Granite sits and suns itself up atop a pretty road with sweeping views of the Continental Divide. Lizards crawl over its rubble. The massive tumbled stone blocks, fallen timbers, and twisted iron of its huge mill loom above the wreckage like some melancholy Mayan ruin. Only the impressive lofted Miners Union Hall, the mill superintendent's splendorous stone office, a little jail, a frame hospital, and a few cribs from the red-light district, Silk Stocking Row, remain reasonably intact. Of the bank there remains only the collapsing vault, strewn with forgotten records.

Since Black Creek to the west has been torn down very recently and Georgetown and Southern Cross to the south are both sparse and spoiled, I gave them short shrift, crossed the Divide, followed the elegiacally beautiful Big Hole River west and proceeded into Idaho. Rejoining the most direct route to Salmon City near Lost Trail Pass, one shortly strikes the Salmon River again. From there the city is 22 miles upriver.

For breakfast I picked out the Chatterbox Cafe, the best of Salmon City's false-front buildings. White-painted, neatly curtained at the windows, the Chatterbox has to rank right up there as one of the best of the old-time cafes anywhere in the Rockies. One feels certain that no one would look askance if a customer entered in derby or button shoes.

Encouraged by this amiable atmosphere, I asked the nice gray-haired lady behind the counter whether she had ever heard of an old saloon in town with a skull behind the bar. Nominally, at least, I am a great believer in the kind of serendipity that enables one to select by hunch the most intriguing looking building or person in a place and get the most recondite question answered there. It doesn't always work.

The lady wrinkled her forehead. Then she smiled. "Oh,

that would have been at the old Buckhorn Saloon," she said brightly. I blinked. Funny feeling to have what you thought of as a perfectly mythological story, told to you in a distant place, suddenly materialize into a chunk of reality at precisely the proper location.

"The Buckhorn was torn down years ago," she continued. Wasn't *that* frustrating! Although not surprising. Anyone young enough to be forced to do his prospecting for history in the 1960s is always arriving places a little too late.

"If you want to know about that," the Chatterbox lady added helpfully, "ask old John Snook. He's our oldest citizen. You'll find him in the big white house just beyond the Conoco station. He's a very nice man—I'm sure he'll be happy to see you—and he still remembers things very clearly."

I drove down to the big Victorian house on Main Street, rang the bell, and knocked on the door. For a long time, there was no answer. Suddenly the door was yanked open. A tall straight man with a vigorous shock of white hair stood there, blue and clear of eye, steady of hand. I explained my mission and recounted the barest details of the strange Idaho sequel to the Bender story, stripping it of the lurid parts and trying to make it as dry and believable as possible so as not to expose myself as a credulous outlander.

"Oh, yes," John Snook said matter-of-factly. "It was my father who caught the man supposed to be Bender. Father was the first deputy sheriff of Lemhi County," Snook began, after he had sat me down in a big overstuffed chair in his parlor. "John Ramey was the sheriff, but he spent most of his time up at Leesburg, which was a roaring gold camp then—murders and brawls all the time. Anyway, Indians found the body of a boy—a miner, but still just a boy—in an eddy of the river between here and Challis. There was nothing but a trail to Challis, no road at all, even when I was a young man. I don't even remember what the boy's

140

name was. The killer stole the fellow's gray mare, and then made the mistake of stopping in Challis. People recognized the mare and told my father—his name was John, too—about it. After a long chase, my father and some other Salmon men caught the murderer, arrested him, and brought him back to Salmon City. He committed suicide in the Salmon jail. They found him lying there with his wrists gashed. I was only a small boy, but I still remember the excitement. I can remember Bender saying, 'I didn't kill that boy,' and Ramey saying, 'We're going to send you back where you killed a lot of people.' I guess he knew then that he had been recognized.

"Doc Kenney was doctor here then, and he gave the body to his brother to have as a skeleton. Someone eventually put the skull in the Buckhorn.

"Donald Martin, the sheriff here for years, knows more of the story. He's looked into the old records. Donald lives right up there on the hill. I'm sure he'd be happy to tell you about it. Why don't you stop and see him?"

All in a fever to learn more now, I arranged to see Martin, a handsome, amiable, gray-haired, crew-cut man living in a neat bungalow above Salmon.

"Yes, I know something about Bender, the man who ran those murder-farms back in Kansas," Martin said. ". . . if it was Bender, and I think it probably was. He was seen in Challis with a young man. They left together for Salmon on the trail on the opposite side of the river from the present road. They must have camped at a certain creek along the way. Both the trail and the campsite are still there, if you knew where to look.

"The old man appeared, alone, in Salmon. He had a horse shod and his laundry washed. The laundrywoman noticed small spots of blood on one shirt, but didn't think too much of it. Bender finished his errands and left town.

"Shortly afterward, an Indian named Mouse reported to Deputy Sheriff John Snook—five thousand to six thousand men were over the hill in Leesburg then, you know, and the sheriff spent most of his time over there, leaving Salmon to the deputy—that he had found a body in a creek. Its head was split with an ax.

"A mail carrier identified the corpse as the fellow seen with the old man. Snook and two men tracked the murderer up the old Agency Creek stage road going east and pursued him all the way to beyond Dillon, Montana. [Dillon, county seat of Beaverhead County, still big, wild country west of the Ruby Range, would be at least one hundred miles east of Salmon by the tortuous old roads.] They surrounded him there and tied him to a horse to bring him back. That's a painful way to travel, but he was so dangerous and acting up so bad that they couldn't take any chances. On the way back, they stopped at Bannack.

"You know what a wild town Bannack always was. [Bannack, whose raw realities all but surpassed western ghost town legend, is one of the most famous camps of all. It had vigilantes, Indian uprisings, lynchings, and bonanza opulences in extravagant profusion.] Well, it was wilder yet, because this happened to be the Fourth of July and all the miners were getting likkered up. Snook feared a lynching, so he left town, sneaking his prisoner out before dark.

"All the way back, Snook got to thinking. He had seen posters, and realized that the old man fit Bender's description well. So did the mode of murder. Almost afraid to say it, he told the other two men his suspicion. They had been thinking exactly the same thing.

"When they got back to Salmon, Snook told the man he thought he was Bender. Next morning he was found dead in a pool of his own blood.

"Here there are two stories. John Junior says he saw the old man with his wrists slashed, a suicide. Charlie, his brother, says the prisoner chopped at his ankle, trying to escape. I lean toward Charlie's version, myself.

"Anyway, it was summertime, so the body couldn't be shipped to Kansas. Snook buried it in an alkali patch up the

142

hill, hoping the alkali would preserve the body. But the guard he had posted left his post, attracted by excitement in the town below. A horse race was going on. They used to run them right down the main street, and lots of money changed hands. Taking advantage of this, old 'Doc' Kenney and his brother stole the body. [Cadavers and skeletons were awfully hard to come by back then, and doctors often resorted to grave robbing.]

"They tried cooking off the meat in a vat to get the skeleton, but it stank so they couldn't stand it. Then they put the corpse on the dirt roof of the shack up at Seventeen Mile House on that same Agency Creek road, hoping the magpies would clean it up. But the birds flew off with several vertebrae, ruining the skeleton.

"The rest of the skeleton stayed up there for a long time. Finally the skull tumbled down off the roof. Happening to pass by, Snook—who had stopped being deputy and gone into the freighting business—picked it up. He had it mounted on the lead pole of his wagon for years.

"The day he delivered his last freight, he stopped in front of the Buckhorn Saloon. The owner, Jack Black, came out. "I'll give you a quart of whiskey for that skull,' he said. Snook, who was a teetotaler, said, 'I have no use for the whiskey and no use for the skull, but I'll give it to you for nothing.'

"The Buckhorn was closed up during Prohibition, but both before and after, I saw that skull there many a time. In later years, the old Buckhorn had many different owners, and one must have taken it with him when he left, because the skull finally just disappeared. Maybe it still exists somewhere.

"Was the man really Bender? John Snook was sure of it, and so were the others. I knew all of them and they were sober, cautious men. I believe them."

There it was. One of the more extravagant stories since men went west for gold, and it was practically all true. How many other all but unknown stories like this are there around the West? How many will die with the last of the Sylvan Harts?

These two men alone, Martin and Snook, have many another tale demanding to be retold. Snook's history is especially interesting. "I'll soon have been here ninety-one years, the twentieth of October," he says, still vigorous and troubled only by dimming eyesight. "I'm the oldest native left in the county. Nora Whitlow is five years older but not a native.

"As a small boy, I remember helping my father drive cattle to the Leesburg slaughter house. It was an exciting place for a boy, as you can imagine—all men, a lot of them Chinamen. When one of the Chinamen died, the others used to ship the body back to China, out by stage and then on by railroad and sailing ship. Salmon itself was half Chinamen, and mostly log cabins with dirt roofs, when Leesburg was going.

"Leesburg was still going pretty strong when my dad came in, freighting machinery, lumber, and supplies. My father first came to Virginia [City]. He drove an ox team all the way from Ioway in '62 and '63. Then he used to freight in from Corinne [wicked Corinne, Utah, most crimson of all the railheads] when it was western terminus of the Union Pacific, before the meeting of rails at Promontory. That was a trip of many days. He also used to carry the mails on a packhorse between here and there.

"I started freighting in 1907 myself. It used to take sixteen horses to haul a boiler up the ten-mile hill up to Leesburg. Charles Goff, here in Salmon, has a lot of pictures of Leesburg mining, back in the eighties."

Snooks was interested by a question I chanced to ask about the Thunder Mountain mining district south of Sylvan's place on the Salmon. "We have the only baby ever born at Thunder Mountain," he said, "Bill Hanmer, the postmaster here for years. It was a good thing for him his father was a doctor.

144

"Corny Sullivan, another oldtimer, said things shook all the time at Thunder. The Indians called it 'Mountain That Shakes.' They were quite superstitious about it."

Snook also remembered the old Pittsburg & Gilmore, one of the last-built, least economic, and most ephemeral of Western ghost railroads, a railway from Armstead, Montana, to Salmon City, Idaho. "The Pittsburg & Gilmore, with a tunnel you can still see on the Rocky Mountain divide, came in here in 1909," he said. "The intention was to go down the Salmon and connect all the way to the West Coast. Since you've been down the Salmon, you known why they didn't. I rode the P & G and shipped cattle and horses both. Highway 28 was built on the old roadbed. The depot used to be down where the Intermountain Lumber Company stands now." When he took me down to Salmon's little museum, where he is a frequent and well-loved visitor, Snook pointed out a picture of the driving of the P & G's golden spike.

At the museum, Snook could point with authority at a photograph of the first women to come into the valley by covered wagon and say, "My mother, Emily Ellis, is in that picture." Or walk past a photograph of early Salmon and mention, "My mother's father built the first hotel here, the International." He could indicate a nice early false front ("Here's Chet Mathison's livery stable. My father built it and sold it to Chet") or admire a collection of antique campaign buttons and admit modestly, "In 1908, I was the first Republican ever to carry Gibbonsville."

Snook was an Idaho representative in 1909 and 1921 and warden of the state penitentiary for seven years, but by far the most absorbing of his experiences relate to his time as deputy U.S. Marshal at Juneau, Alaska, during the Klondike rush: "It's funny how some little incident can change your whole life. In '97, I trailed some rustlers who slaughtered my heifer five miles up Kay Mountain. Got them dead to rights, too. I had all the evidence—the bloody saddle, the tracks of the corks on the soles of their shoes. At the trial, when I presented all this, Jim Shoup was very impressed. He said he wished to God I was old enough to be appointed his deputy, because he had just been appointed U.S. Marshal in Skagway, Alaska. I told him I was just old enough to qualify, having turned twenty-one. So Alaska was my first job of law enforcement.

"I went to Dyea as deputy in the winter of 1897, through '98. Dyea folded up when they built the White Pass Railroad, and I became deputy marshal at Skagway from 1900 to 1904. I helped dig forty-nine bodies out of a snowslide in Yukon Territory in spring of '98—including five nameless men, evidently fugitives from the U.S., all roped together. There were a lot of nameless men in the Klondike, and almost all of them were fugitives.

"See that little finger I can't straighten out? On the twenty-sixth of April, 1898, a man tried to kill me seven miles above Dyea on the Chilcoot Trail. I managed to deflect the gun enough so the bullet hit only this finger. I had him under arrest at the time, and he was trying to escape."

Snook even ran across the notorious Soapy Smith, gambler and outlaw chief first of roaring Creede, Colorado, and then of the still rougher Klondike. "I took Soapy Smith and his bunch over to Sitka—I had charge of the jail there—after he had killed Frank Reed," the old man said animatedly. "They had a citizens' meeting down at the wharf at Skagway. Frank, the city engineer, was guarding the meeting. Soapy's first cartridge merely snapped, the second got Frank right through the heart. I had to take Smith to Sitka because the U.S. commissioner in Skagway only had authority to sentence for six months or less."

Snook took several photographs off his mantel. The first showed Soapy Smith and his gang aboard a parlor car. The second was a picture of White Pass on June 16, 1899, with Deputy Snook included in a group riding the White Pass & Yukon narrow gauge in its first year of full operation. The third showed the steamer landing at Dyea with a classic wooden boom town in the background, its most prominent buildings the Glacier Hotel and the Glacier Restaurant. Another pictured dogteams on the Dyea River and another, Fourth of July at Skagway in 1901. Others recorded the Skagway basketball team (Snook was captain in 1901 and 1902), the fire company, the newspaper office.

But the most remarkable of all was the picture of a solid line of men climbing savage Chilcoot Pass in the winter of '97–'98 on the way to Dawson, British Columbia, and the goldfields. Taken from a distance great enough to show the high pass from bottom to top—great enough so that no individual figure could be picked out—the photograph showed a thin black line, dense and continuous, stretching from the valley below to the summit thousands of feet higher. The landscape was entirely white with ice and snow. Not a tree or a bush showed. Yet, chillingly like a mile-long procession of black ants swarming to honey, thousands of men climbed through the deep snows of this bleak, hostile land.

I told Snook it was a truly historic picture. "Yes, I guess it is," he said. "Thirteen Mounties were stationed at the foot of that pass solely to inspect the miners' food and supplies, yet many men died."

After he had showed me and told me all I asked, and invited me to come again, Snook had only one question of his own. Who had sent me to him? I told him. "Oh, yes, that would be Violet Richardson at the Chatterbox," he said. "Withington, really, but I still think of her as a Richardson."

I felt quite grateful to Violet Richardson-Withington, and, steeped in all that I had learned, began the trek back to Five Mile Bar.

⋘⋘ 12

"I DON'T DOUBT THE man at Salmon was a Bender," Sylvan said after reflecting on the evidence I presented him. "The *modus operandi* and the reactions were like the Benders, for one thing. But I don't think he was *the* Old Man Bender. I heard the most famous family of the tribe— that is, he and Kate and the boy—were killed and put in a well in our part of eastern Kansas."

Authentic a source as Buckskin is on many such matters, I nevertheless felt inclined to give greater weight to Snook and Martin as more proximate sources in this Bender case.

Taking mock offense, Bill broad-humoredly declined to risk his analytical reputation on yet another story, this one the poignant account of Annie MacIntyre of Rocky Bar. He was interested, however, by the version I told him. Buckskin, you see, not only lives near ghost towns (those are relatively common) but near a whole ghost county, which is rare. Old Alturas County, 19,180 miles square, once comprised all of Idaho south of the Rocky Mountain divide, east of the 39th meridian, west of approximately the 35th, and north of the Snake River. When, after the gold rush had died, Alturas's population slowly sank so low as to render it a hollow land much bigger than Switzerland, it was gradually dismembered and the pieces absorbed by neighboring counties. Now an isolated ghost town, Rocky Bar was seat of the totally vanished county.

Into booming Rocky Bar on the Fourth of July, 1864, came four-year-old Annie, carried on her father's back. Steve McIntyre, owner of the rich Golden Star mine, was soon killed in a street fight, but the tiny girl with huge brown eyes lived to become a tall, pretty woman and the owner of Rocky Bar's most prominent lodging house. Legend says she never turned away a hungry or exhausted man, yet she was tough-willed enough to often quiet a rowdy customer by pulling out a pistol and firing a few bullets into the wall.

Just Plain Dutch, genial last resident and unofficial custodian of the town, owns the last surviving hotel building in Rocky Bar, a spectral edifice still tattered with plush and ornate wallpaper and mahogany. His mother, he says, stayed for a while in the hotel when she first came to the gold country. There is reason to believe this is Annie's establishment.

In 1898, then thirty-eight but still very much in her prime, Anne MacIntyre left Atlanta, Idaho—another ghostly and even remoter town—to return with another woman to Rocky Bar. It was a fine day, and they stopped to chat with a mail carrier who happened to pass them on the way. When the carrier reached town, he chanced to mention that he had seen them. Those happenstances were their partial salvation. A freakish snowstorm sprang up. The women never arrived. Days later, the rescue party found Annie crawling around in circles on bare hands and knees over the snow, uttering guttural, animal-like sounds.

When the searchers finally located her companion, they found her frozen stiff, covered, pitifully, with Annie's undergarments. Once, as they ascended steep Bald Mountain, the log-like corpse slipped out of their numb hands and rolled all the way to the bottom.

Taken back to Atlanta, where a doctor was still eighty miles distant, Annie was filled full of whiskey and tied

150

down while her legs were amputated with a jackknife and saw. She survived to run her restaurant, cheerfully, for years afterward and came to be known as Peg Leg Annie.

Twenty of those years she lived with an Italian who went by the assumed name of Henry Longheme and operated the saloon next door. In the 1920s, when Longheme decided to revisit his native Italy, she gave him $12,000—her entire savings—to be deposited in San Francisco. She never heard from him again. To her death, she loyally clung to the belief that Longheme had been robbed and killed.

The story of Peg Leg Annie—apocryphal though it may be—couldn't help but remind Sylvan of Bert Churchill, a former neighbor who built the vertiginous switchback trail from Dixie over Churchill Mountain down into the Salmon River gorge and who settled on the north bank of the river on a bar not far distant from Hart's place. Churchill had an unloving wife and, in place of a hand lost in an accident of some sort, an iron hook attached to the stump with a kind of leather harness. Neither improved his disposition.

One day when Churchill was crossing the Salmon with two other men, their rowboat capsized. Somehow the three managed to clamber onto a big boulder located in mid-stream above Richardson Rapids, and rescuers were able to throw a rope to each in turn. When they came to Churchill, the last, he merely grasped the rope with hand and hook instead of tying it around him. Pulled out into the vicious current of the flooding river, Churchill felt a sickening sensation. Squeaking, stretching, and then snapping, the straps fastening the hook, weakened by long use and rotted with age, tore in two. Unable to hold on with one hand, he was swept down into the roaring rapids. "Good!" his wife screamed in glee. "There goes the meanest man in Idaho!"

Hart remembered Churchill as a trapper, a very ambitious one. "He ran a trapline and made as much as thirty miles a day on skis," Sylvan said approvingly. "Every pioneer, particularly one as diligent as that, must be stubborn, and a woman often confuses stubbornness as meanness. No one here ever said Churchill was mean, but I think there was a lot of iron in him."

And as for the iron attached to him, if someone someday finds among the river rocks a rusted hook with dangling straps of leather, the finder will know to whom the grisly artifact belonged: Sylvan's onetime neighbor on the Salmon.

The extraordinary way in which tragedy annealed the mettle of the Salmon country pioneers has no better illustration than in the story Sylvan and I had both heard of Three-Fingered Smith, father of Hart's good friend Henry. An early settler on the South Fork, which joins the main river at Mackay Bar, the elder Smith acquired his name by getting bit by a rattlesnake. With a fine disdain for half measures, he picked up an ax and chopped off the two fingers that had been bitten.

Smith's trials only began with that small incident. Some time afterward, a son who carried mail to various mining camps sat down one winter day to rest and froze to death. Then Smith's wife ran away with a seaman from San Francisco. Worse, marauding Indians ran off his horses. When Smith rounded up help to pursue the redskins (there is no record of his having bothered about the woman), they killed three of his comrades and left Smith for dead. He survived only by crawling, badly wounded, to a friend's cabin thirty-five miles away.

What a modern man might have taken as good excuses to die, Smith saw as opportunity to start a new life. Recovered, he moved to Florence, where he found a rich strike. Thereupon he returned to Warren, where he spent—legend has it—$100,000 in one hundred days by the simple expedient of buying saloons and turning them over to his friends. If they didn't like the brand of liquor in one saloon, he'd buy another. When that first fortune was gone, he mended his financial shorts by promptly striking another bonanza, relieved himself of this the same way, and died a lusty, unpitiable pauper.

Oddly, though at various widely separate times, Sylvan had talked about both Three-Fingered and Henry Smith, I did not for some time connect the famous gold rush pioneer with Hart's friend on the South Fork. When I finally figured out the relationship and wrote to Hart asking him to tell more about the Smiths, he was pleased to reply with a remarkable, sprawling epistle written with quill pen in broad green strokes across the length of several sheets of paper.

Since I had written to him from Manhattan in the dead of winter, when he is thoroughly snowed in, this was no routine correspondence. Particularly because Sylvan had not been expecting my letter, I first had to wait until snow and trail conditions were such that travel was feasible and then until Hart felt motivated to snowshoe down to Mackay Bar to pick up whatever mail might have accumulated over the last month or so. If Sylvan were not too deeply absorbed in a wood- or copper-working project, he could then ponder his reply and write it out. Finally, the next time the snow was right, he could trek back to the bar downriver. In a week or two, the mail plane would pick up his answer. In this case, the whole process took about eight weeks.

The letter began with the salutation *How*:

"I must have told you Henry Smith was the son of Three-fingered Smith when I showed you the rifle he gave me," Sylvan inscribed, and added a version that Smith Sr. had had one of the missing fingers shot off with a muzzle-loading shotgun.

"Three-fingered had all his gold on a mule in a gun boot when he left Florence," he continued. "One hundred thousand dollars would weigh 300 pounds, but they put 400 pounds then on a good mule. Henry laughed when he found his frozen brother: he thought it was a good joke on him. Henry told me his father took three .45 to .50 caliber bullets during that Indian fight and needed a couple of months to recover. Three-fingered had told his horse hunters, 'Those trees weren't there when we came by be-

153

fore,' but it was almost too late. The Indians dropped the trees they had been carrying for camouflage and started shooting. Smith waded the Secesh River, wounded as he was, and his mail carrier friend found him next day. It is true, yes, that he had the richest claims in both Florence and Warren.

"Incidentally, Warren Smith, Henry's other brother, was named after tinhorn Warren of Warren's [gambler James Warren, who had the first big strike at the town named for him]. He paid his workers at his mine on Warren Summit every night so they could go to town and spend it."

I had also asked Sylvan for certain particulars on the Hart family, in light of some discoveries I had made from genealogical sources about its history in Revolutionary times. Not an ancestor worshiper, Sylvan has no formal knowledge of his lineage, but he does know most of the best stories about many of his forebears. Thus, in his reply, he rambled briefly and interestingly, telling of Nancy Hart, who cooked her last turkey when the Tories came in order to lure them into a rebel trap, and of John Henry Hart of Iola, one of the earliest Kansans. He talked too of the related Tucks ("a tuck is a small slim sword") and of how one of the first of the family was Sir Brian Tuck, secretary to Henry VIII and Cardinal Wolsey during their intrigue-ridden times.

Questions answered, Sylvan turned with delight to sharing the sense of winter spent in the far snow-locked reaches of the land. "A bighorn sheep has been watching me dig a cellar," he wrote. "A mountain lion has investigated my bomb shelter and put one foot inside. I made some more cherrywood dishes, and I have been making jewelry and silversmithing."

When spring came, Hart said, he thought he would go outside and give a talk at a high school to counterindoctrinate the young. It was pleasant to contemplate the roaring sensation he would be, this old mountain lion of a man in buckskins at a modern high school. At the request of friends who are teachers, I have talked to a few classes, from sixth grade to senior level, about Sylvan and some similar survivals of America's past. Attention is always rapt. Hands wave like a pondful of rushes, questions come like bullets, and there is a touching excitement as the young discover, many for the first time, that the mythic American way of life remains a viable alternative to the present.

"Looks like you need to make another trip to Idaho," Hart concluded. "Visit here if you can." The letter was signed, in large green script, "Buckskin Bill."

«‹«‹«Epilogue

As I read the last of Sylvan Hart's letter, sitting high above Manhattan, thoughts of the beauty and deep-rooted peace of the empty Idaho wildnesses, together with the reminders of the Harts's romantic history, freshened the memory of a very recent trip to Hopewell, New Jersey, easier to visit than Five Mile Bar, yet evocative of the little-known Hart legend. The old Baptist church still stands over the burying ground where John Hart lies, a slightly idolatrous little old lady still treasures a small glass vial containing a few wisps of the patriot's hair, and the whole town visibly remembers 1776. John Hart's homestead, although rebuilt after an 1820 fire, remains very much of that or an earlier period. One can stand in the lane in front of it and easily reconstruct the feeling that sent more than twenty patriots on this three-mile stretch of road off to fight the Revolution. One can look at the house, and the hill behind it, and reconstruct June of 1778. As Washington marched to the Battle of Monmouth, Jesse and Nathaniel Hart guided the army east from Coryell's Ferry on the Delaware. Fully aware of the harm an encampment would do, they led the weary Continentals to their father's farm. The encampment here did tramp down crops, burn fences for fuel, and sully Tommy's Pond, but the Harts bore the damage cheerfully and without complaint. They knew,

157

perhaps, that the very mainstream of world history does not run through your dooryard without muddying it a little.

One can thus expand one's own consciousness with others' memory because Hopewell is still mostly intact. Protected by wealth and lying just off the New York–Philadelphia corridor, it will survive another few years. But within an ambling walk the sores of overpopulation and undereducation begin. Within a short drive is the continuous reeking rot that has driven most of the Harts of America westward.

I then looked down to where the Hudson River ran foul with waste and sewage past the rat infested wharves of the same New Jersey. Black soot—accumulated residue of an annual sootfall of sixty tons per square mile—lay thick as always on every surface. Black clouds of burning garbage billowed upwards. The air, a dirty orange at the tops of car-choked canyons, shaded down to a reddish brown at the bottom of sulfurous defiles. Inch-long cockroaches crawled in every luxury apartment building. Scurrying, shoving humans snarled, spat, and swore in crud-caked subways. The relatively rich and stable fought for creeping cabs and hoped their barred, bolted, police-locked, bespiked semi-slums had not been burglarized yet again, or rode cheek to jowl through Harlem to suburban sanctuary. The utterly alienated sat stuporously in a hundred thousand crack-walled hutches.

No one ever talks about the famous Cornell University psychological study that classed a mere 18.5 percent of mid-town New Yorkers as mentally well. But people do speak, uneasily, almost in whispers, of the now-notorious—at least in the underground of the concerned—study of rat over-population, in which laboratory rodents progressively exhibit an uncannily human pattern of collective nervous breakdown.

If there were only one human behavioral sink like New York, it would be merely a cruel but interesting social laboratory. But the population of the United States quadruples within a man's lifetime—50 million in 1880, 100 million in 1918, 150 million in 1950, 200 million in 1967. Regard for the individual—his feelings, his opinions, his attempts to achieve meaning, and finally his life—necessarily attenuates and disappears. To whom do the mass communications and wholesale education really speak? Law and representative government sink under the weight of numbers. Even where one finds communities and regions that are relatively clean reservoirs of calm and integrity, the less diseased inhabitants must inoculate themselves with hostility, suspicion, and selfishness to guard against outside carriers of the infection of hate, fear, and greed.

Still, for a time, beyond the reach of mass media's last captive electron, there are oases of unpollution.

I thought of the many feet of soft snow, white and dry as new linen paper, spread across the whole wilderness of Idaho. Boldly engraved on that whiteness are the dark pines and the fine tracery of bare branches. Crisp, sharp tracks of elk and lynx and mountain sheep cross the snowy flats like lines of clear print. Following one of those lines, paralleling its clean-cut characters with the slurred, scuffing marks of snowshoes, is an old man who reads the tracks like a book, like poetry, like the words of a formal invitation. He is an old man with a beard red at the sides, white at the chin, and gray at the tip, wearing a black bearskin cap and home-sewn elk-leather boots, on homemade wicker snowshoes, and in his eyes there is the joy of living.

The rivers and creeks run black and cold, the winter air is clearer and purer than ever, the man is utterly alone and utterly free. When snow covers the trails and blue-white chunks of ice swirl down the swift river, the twentieth century ceases to exist. When the trails are mantled and the river impassable, only the sure and strong and determined can reach him. No man truly of this decade can touch him then, for the decade is confused and weak and aimless.

When one pale plume of blue smoke curls from his chimney, it dissolves into the endless thistled eden that was

159

the realm of Jedediah Smith, and the Nez Percé and Shoshone before him, and the lost civilization of the Basketmakers before them. The material missionaries of a new civilization have yet to come, bringing hope and promise of a new Canaan, of an emerald isle transplanted and purified, of a Newer England, of a more beautiful and more fragile flower grafted onto a stronger stock. When this true civilization comes (if it comes), an aristocracy of common men will discuss law and letters and arts and philosophy on shady village greens and in spacious wooden-grecian temples of houses and churches, schools and meeting halls. Then these last extremities of distance, altitude, brightness of light, lightness of air and glory of surrounding scene will finally defeat the false priests who bow and pray to the neon god.

Meantime, the first man on the ground, the pioneer, awaits the first vivid translucent pastels of bud and leaf and flower of a certain springtime. He awaits that future with confidence and calm, as quiet and sure as the melting of the snows into ice-hidden rills and rivulets, as purposeful and powerful as their gathering into the inexorable River of No Return. For in the country whose light still shines pure on pristine mountains there is, yet, a future.